Fathers & Daughters
& Sports

Fathers & Daughters & Sports

FEATURING JIM CRAIG, CHRIS EVERT, MIKE GOLIC, DORIS KEARNS GOODWIN, SALLY JENKINS, STEVE RUSHIN, BILL SIMMONS, AND OTHERS

INTRODUCTION BY
Rebecca Lobo

BALLANTINE BOOKS NEW YORK

ESPN
BOOKS

Published in the United States by ESPN Books, an imprint of ESPN, Inc.,
New York, and Ballantine Books, an imprint of The Random House Publishing
Group, a division of Random House, Inc., New York.

BALLANTINE and colophon are registered trademarks of Random House, Inc.
The ESPN Books name and logo are registered trademarks of ESPN, Inc.

Permissions information can be found in the acknowledgments,
starting on page 250.

Library of Congress Cataloging-in-Publication Data
Fathers & daughters & sports : featuring Jim Craig, Chris Evert, Mike Golic,
Doris Kearns Goodwin, Sally Jenkins, Steve Rushin, Bill Simmons, and others /
introduction by Rebecca Lobo.
p. cm.
ISBN 978-0-345-52083-8 (hardcover : alk. paper)
eBook ISBN 978-0-345-52207-8
1. Sports—United States. 2. Fathers and daughters—United States   I. Title.
GV583.F37 2010
796.0973—dc22   2010009584

Printed in the United States of America on acid-free paper

www.ballantinebooks.com
www.espnbooks.com

2 4 6 8 9 7 5 3

Book design by Karin Batten

CONTENTS

INTRODUCTION

⌇⌇

Rebecca Lobo

I used to be the Hat With the Kid Under It. That's what my dad called me. He had nicknames for everyone and everything—Dickensian names for pets and offspring. Our guinea pig, he named Pinnywigg. My brother was Pigglypear. And I, the youngest of his three children, was the Hat With the Kid Under It.

The hat that wore me everywhere as an eight-year-old was a green Oakland A's model. I wasn't an A's fan. We were all Red Sox fans in western Massachusetts. I just inherited my brother's old Little League cap. I was a tomboy through and through. I fished, shot hoops, and played catch. And I did those with my dad. Always with my dad. And not just because the nearest neighbor kids were a quarter of a mile away.

There was nothing better than a catch with Dad on a Saturday afternoon. I would beg him to throw the ball with me in the front yard after he was done mowing the lawn. I'd fetch our gloves and wait for him to finish his attempt at making our grass look like the outfield at Fenway Park. I wanted to be Carlton Fisk. I also wanted to be Larry Bird and Mark Bavaro. When my mom said, "You can be whatever you want when you grow up," I told her, "I want to play in the NFL." Mom said, "Anything but *that.*"

Dad didn't say much of anything. After putting the push mower back in the garage, his brow covered in sweat, he would toss the ball with me. Every time I threw the ball in his direction, he said: "Step and follow through," one of a handful of instructional catchphrases I would hear a lot over the years. Literally a *catch* phrase, it occurs to me now. Whenever he declared our catch over, whether it was after five minutes or thirty-five, it was too soon. For me, not for him. I think now he just wanted a beer.

For most of my childhood, our driveway wasn't paved. It was covered in gravel and not ideal for basketball. You could have the best handle in the world and still lose control of the ball if it hit a rogue stone. But after the basketball hoop was cemented into the ground near the garage, that driveway was our heavenly playground. I spent countless hours shooting and dribbling and playing H-O-R-S-E. I would use the toe of my shoe to draw a perforated arc in the gravel for Around the

World. And Dad would take that transcontinental driveway journey with me. Every time I shot the ball from straightaway, he called out, "On your toes!" Depending on who won, the arc would mirror my face: smiling or frowning.

In fifth grade, my teacher told me that I needed to dress more like a girl and act more like a girl. She didn't approve of my Giants jersey or my playing with the boys at recess. When I got home from school that day, I shot hoops until my parents returned from work. Both teachers themselves, they were appropriately angry when I told them what had happened. Mom had me removed from the classroom. Dad and I just continued to play catch, our therapy—or at least mine.

Perhaps he didn't know what to say to his six-foot, sixth-grade daughter. Six-four if you counted the hairdo. This was the Heyday of Hairspray, the eighties, the Golden Age of Metal Bands. My school photos looked a lot like Eddie Van Halen in drag. Then again, at the time Eddie Van Halen looked a lot like Eddie Van Halen in drag.

As I got older, Dad spent countless hours driving me to camps, practices, and AAU tournaments: West Virginia, Tennessee, Louisiana. Every spring and summer when I was in high school, our Saturday afternoons were devoted to hour-long drives to and from AAU practice. The drive was usually silent—or would have been, if Dad didn't always have the radio in his Toyota pickup tuned to the classic rock station. At some point on every drive—no matter the song—he would say, "Listen to that bass line. That's a *great* bass line." As a teenager, I would roll my eyes. Looking back, it makes me laugh to think how awkward it must have been for him, desperate for something to say to his teenage daughter, by then fully six-foot-four. Six-eight if you counted the hat I wore in marching band. If I wanted to be the world's tallest alto saxophonist, that was fine with Dad.

If he was happy that I chose to play basketball, he never explicitly said so. But I know he was happy. He never missed one of my high school games. He didn't miss any of my home games at the University of Connecticut. When I played in South Korea with the USA junior national team after my sophomore year in college, he was there. When our unbeaten UConn team won the national championship in Minneapolis in 1995, he was there. When my Olympic team won gold in Atlanta in 1996, he was in the stands. And every time I stepped to the free-throw line—during my high school, college, Olympic, and pro careers—he would wait for the hush that precedes a free throw and shout, "On your toes!"

In the last year of my WNBA career, I would stand at that line as a twenty-nine-year-old married woman and listen for my father's unmistakable voice, cutting across the distance at Madison Square Garden or the Mohegan Sun Arena. It had been twenty years since our games on the pebble driveway, but little had changed. I still got incredible joy from sharing sports with my dad. My happiness was still my father's first concern. And I still needed no more words from him than "On your toes!"

My toes. The toes of my high-tops no longer wore the dust of Around the World. But thanks to Dad's endless support, my high-tops had taken me there.

Speaking of toes: My middle name is Rose, and as I grew—and my feet grew to size 12s—he gave me another nickname, Rebecca Rose Monkeytoes.

In locker rooms, I came to realize that nicknames are a sign of affection. By that standard, no one was more loved than I. A year after retiring from professional basketball, I gave birth to a daughter. She is my father's first granddaughter, and he has been wrapped around her finger since day one. She is almost five now and has a special bond with "Dampa." When she rode her bike without training wheels for the first time or swam at the Y without a life vest, she couldn't wait to show him. She badgers him to go fishing and has a pink baseball glove for catch. Whenever she goes to visit him, my dad gets out his ancient and filthy New York Giants hat that he inherited when his own father, a Giants football fanatic, passed away.

Dad puts it on his granddaughter's head. The hat rests on her ears. When he tells my daughter, "You're the Hat With the Kid Under It," he has no idea how close I am to tears.

⸙

But that's just the story of my dad and me. Other daughters, other fathers, have their own sports tales to tell, and this delightful anthology reflects a wide variety of both perspectives and sports.

You'll read Chris Evert's tribute to her father and feel Dan Shaughnessy's delight in watching his daughters play softball. You'll laugh as Bernie Lincicome describes what it's like to be a horse-show dad and marvel at the way Ashley Force Hood and her father express their love at more than 300 mph. You'll return to the night that the daughters of Muhammad Ali and Joe Frazier fought, and you'll be there when an NBA legend tries to connect with the daughter he never knew.

Title IX gave millions of women opportunities they never had before. As this book shows, it also gave fathers and daughters a wealth of material. Enjoy.

REBECCA LOBO *won the 1995 Naismith National Player of the Year Award after leading the University of Connecticut women's basketball team to its first national championship. She was the youngest member of the 1996 gold-medal-winning Olympic basketball team. After seven seasons in the WNBA, she now works as a basketball analyst and reporter for ESPN. She lives in Connecticut with her husband, Steve Rushin, and their three children.*

Fathers & Daughters
& Sports

Q: Who's tougher than a former NFL defensive tackle?
A: His daughter.

WATER PROOF

~~~

Mike Golic with Andrew Chaikivsky

When my daughter, Sydney, was ten years old, she told my wife, Chris, and me that she wanted to play lacrosse. She had grown up watching her two older brothers play, and she was eager to try it herself. Great, we told her, and have some fun out there.

She lasted one game. She came off the field, took out her mouthpiece, and vowed never to return.

"This isn't fun, Dad," she explained. "I liked watching Mike and Jake play, but the girls' game is different. They don't let you hit anybody. You can't knock people down." She was visibly disappointed.

~~~

Sydney stands tough, no doubt about it. Her brothers now both play Division I football at Notre Dame, and even though they each have a few years on her, young Sydney constantly mixed it up with them. She stood her ground. She fought back. My daughter is a sweet and charming girl, but if you think you can grab the TV remote away from her while she's watching *Viva La Bam,* you're certainly in for some trouble.

But toughness is never simply about physical strength. It's a mind-set. I've been around athletes my whole life—swimming with the local YMCA team as a kid, wrestling in high school and college, playing in the NFL for nine seasons, working at ESPN—and you begin to see in people the direction they're going to take, how badly they want to succeed and whether or not they have a chance at making it. Very early on, I saw in Sydney something that I had never seen before in someone so young.

She was spending a happy summer swimming and playing soccer when we took a family trip to Notre Dame. Our sons were going for a four-day football camp, and we learned that the athletic department was holding a swimming camp at the same time for girls ages thirteen to eighteen. We had started Sydney with a water-safety course as soon as she was out of the crib, and before long she was picking up strokes like it was second nature. By five, she was competing in swim meets at a country club near our home in Connecticut, and she had been swimming with local teams ever since. But she was only ten years old. Could Sydney attend the Notre Dame camp? we asked. The coaches agreed to let her participate.

We took her to the pool, and I looked over the practice schedule. The distances and sets seemed especially grueling—workouts that would put some football players to shame—and I asked Sydney if she thought she could handle it. She nodded silently, and we kissed her goodbye.

She swam the first session fine, but with the second practice, the distances began to take their toll on her young body. When she climbed out of the pool, I could tell that something was wrong. She looked sad to me, and I asked her if she was okay.

"This is hard, Dad," she said. "Oh God, this is *tough*."

I tried to be encouraging. "The first couple of practices are always the hardest, Sydney. You can do this. You can stick it out."

I looked at my daughter again and saw tears streaking her cheeks. I felt helpless.

"It'll be okay," I said, holding her close in my arms. "We can ask them about easing up on the distances, maybe doing fewer sets."

She pulled away abruptly. "*No*," she said, "I absolutely don't want to do less." She wiped her eyes dry. "I'll be fine." And with that, she turned around and went back into the pool for the next session.

She finished all her sets that day, every lap for every stroke. She didn't cry, didn't come near to getting rattled, never complained. For the first time, I saw an uncommon tenacity in her as she toughed it out for three more days with the other, much older girls. She made it through the entire camp. After the last day's session, she came back to the hotel room, and it all finally hit her.

She lay down on the bed for a quick nap. She slept for fifteen hours straight.

~~~

For a while, Sydney kept up with the soccer, playing goalie for a local travel team. And swimming too. After a very successful soccer season—her team won the state championship—she asked to talk with us about her future. Her future? Sydney was now eleven.

"I can't play soccer anymore," she told us. "I want to swim in college, hopefully at Notre Dame, and I want to make the Olympic trials, maybe even get to the Games someday. I know that to do these things I'm going to need to devote all my time to swimming."

"But we thought you liked soccer?"

"I do like soccer, Dad," she said. "But I *love* swimming."

My wife and I were a little blown away by all this, and we had more than a few discussions about whether or not it was the right thing for her to do. At eleven, she was throwing all her chips into the pot. But I'll be honest: Part of me was beaming with pride. She knew what she had to do, and she was going for it.

It's been three years since Sydney's decision. She's on her course, progressing steadily through the qualifying times at the regional level, the states, the zones, and the sectionals. Now it's on to the Junior Nationals, then the Senior Nationals, and then hopefully the Olympic trials in 2012.

She swims six days a week. On Mondays and Fridays, she swims twice, first thing in the morning and then again at night. She also has three dry-land practices each week, two-hour sessions of treadmill work and strength training. Obviously, she goes to high school too and has kept her grade point average above a 3.5. She's usually done with Friday's homework by Tuesday night.

She seems to thrive on the routine, but there are days when she's literally exhausted. She swims between 50,000 and 60,000 yards each week. Thirty miles every six days.

They call swimming a team sport, but it isn't really. It's just you and the water and thousands of miles of staring at a thick black line at the bottom of the pool. You're alone. In practices you just have to keep swimming, working out the calculus of strokes per lap and stroke rate, and executing every turn perfectly. Win a race or set a personal best and the achievement is all yours. If you fail, though, it's not because the kicker missed a 39-yard field goal. It's all on you.

And so I worry. My daughter is a beautiful five-foot-ten woman now, but she's also my youngest child, my little girl, and sometimes I want to grab her, hold her tight, and ask her if she's okay.

⁓

Last spring, we went with Sydney to Maryland for a sectional meet where she would be swimming in six events, from the 100-yard breaststroke to the 400-yard individual medley. Her final race was the 200-yard backstroke, and she swam it strong, finishing in 2:06.46.

It was the first time that she had achieved a qualifying

time for the Junior Nationals in any event, the next step in reaching her ultimate goal.

When the race was over, we were all on our feet, clapping and cheering for her as she climbed out of the pool. I looked down and saw the smile on my little girl's face, the smile of an athlete in triumph, the smile of a beautiful woman.

MIKE GOLIC *is co-host of ESPN Radio's* Mike & Mike in the Morning *and an analyst for ESPN's NFL coverage. He cowrote* Mike and Mike's Rules for Sports and Life *with his radio partner Mike Greenberg and Andrew Chaikivsky. Golic is a nine-year veteran of the NFL as a defensive tackle and a former captain of the Notre Dame football team.*

Examples of great athletes passing on their genius abound: the Hulls, the Mannings, the Griffeys, the Bryants. Who knew that sportswriting talent also passed between generations?

EXCELLENCE DISGUISED

—⌇⌇—

Sally Jenkins

At some point, your childhood becomes your own property. It's yours alone, to make of it what you will, and there is not a thing that imperious shadow ruler called your father can do about it. But while you were a child, it belonged to him, and he cast it in his terms.

"You're having a happy childhood," my father told me.

"I am?"

"Yes."

"Why?"

"Because I said so."

My father speared another forkful of RavioliOs from my plate and ate them. It was a ritual for him to sit with his three children and share our supper anytime he and my mother went out for the evening, which was frequently. As in, every night of the week. The phone numbers of their favorite restaurants and bars were pasted on the wall by the phone for the babysitter, along with a calendar. Once, someone asked my younger brother what it was like to grow up the son of a sportswriter and author, Dan Jenkins, who was always traveling the world writing prizewinning stories and bestselling books. My brother considered the question.

"They were out every night, and when they came home they went to Europe," he said.

You can see how a girl might want to go into the same line of work.

Somehow my father, despite his globe-circling career and a reputation for high living and enjoying the smartening effects of scotch, managed to provide us with a childhood that was, in fact, happy. How did he accomplish this? For one thing, he was deceptively sober and attentive to his children, and for another he conveyed the message that we shouldn't feel deprived by his frequent absences, because we were lucky to have a father who enjoyed his job. It was important to love one's occupation, he suggested. Not many people cared enough about their living to *want* to do it well. His work, he implied, was a value.

Clearly, he was not a conventional father. He was not a hedge-trimming, lawn-mowing kind of dad. He was not handy around the house or good with a checkbook, and he did not dandle us on his knee, intoning homespun moral wisdom. He was gone on the weekends and home on Tuesdays. He was absent for Thanksgiving (football games) and Easter (the Masters). Every day he drank twenty-two cups of coffee, smoked four packs of cigarettes, and got hate mail from Notre Damers. Nevertheless, I thought he was a better father than nine-tenths of the ones I knew.

"Okay, you kids never got a vote—because kids shouldn't get a vote," he said when I got older. "But while you're totaling up the deficiencies in your childhood, don't forget to mention the vacations in Hawaii and the Park Avenue penthouse."

Mainly, I thought all fathers were the drop-dead funniest guys on earth. The first writing of his I ever read came in the form of picture postcards from distant places. My mother would turn the television to whatever event my father happened to be covering and hand each of us a postcard. "That's where your dad is," she'd say, pointing at the screen. There might be a football game on, which invariably seemed to be played between Nebraska and Oklahoma, or an Olympic ski race, usually won by a skinny Frenchman in tight pants named Jean-Claude Killy.

Italian Alps, Dolomiti di Brenta, 1967

Dear sweet girl,
This is where Daddy eats lunch before he falls down the mountain. Daddy needs a haircut, a shave, and a cheeseburger, but nobody speaks English here.

Be a good little girl and hug your brothers. I love you,

Daddy.

Kitzbühel, Winter Sommersportsplatz, 1967

Daddy drinks lots of wine and eats his soup and cheese. You would have fun here falling down with Daddy and riding the trains. Kiss Momma and your brothers for me.

Even the morning I was born, seven minutes ahead of my twin brother, my father sized up the situation and decided, at arguably the most profound moment of his life, that it was rich with sporty one-liners.

"Girl at 3:50, boy at 3:57," the doctor announced.

To which my father replied, "Kinda heavy, aren't they?"

The dinner hour was always ours. Before my parents went out, he would sit at the kitchen table with his three children, surrounded by their plates and tall glasses of milk. My father would talk to us while he stole bites of our kiddie food. Alphabet soup. Creamed corn. Franks and beans. Stouffer's frozen vegetables.

This was his idea of fatherly advice as we sat at the dinner table: "Don't rob old people," he said.

Around him, his three children would capsize their milk, giggling.

"Daddy?"

"Yes."

"I learned a joke today."

"Tell it."

"What's green and lives in the sea?"

"What?"

"Moby Pickle."

He began laughing helplessly and couldn't stop for the next five minutes, while around him three pajamaed urchins banged their forks on the table with delight.

Many of the stories he wrote, of course, represented absences. But not as many as you might think. He was, despite my brother's joke, a vividly present father. When we got old enough, he often took us with him. His story assignments became family summer vacations. We scampered with impunity through pressrooms and carried hot coffee to him, and we surely must have pestered him, though he never complained of it.

The combined quality and volume of his writing on golf, football, Olympic skiing, and hundreds of other subjects was breathtaking, given that he produced it while also attending school plays, writing checks to orthodontists, mustering private-school tuitions, and lifting the family luggage. All of which he made seem effortless. His fathering style, interestingly, was not much different from his writing style, which is to say, excellence disguised as offhandedness.

Hi, Sal,

In a hurry. Something's about to happen on page 206 I didn't expect. Here's the money for the guns and the grenades. Be careful. Remember how long they held the Hearst girl in custody.

Sweetheart,

This should see you through your next three or four motel stops, pay for the pound of heroin, and help get your friends out of the Turkish prison. How are the hand grenades holding out? Did the bike gang blow up the church as was planned?

As far as I could tell, being a sportswriter the way my father practiced the trade meant grinning to himself as he rattled away on an old Royal typewriter. It meant a constant effort to think about things more plainly, the better to describe them. It meant easy rhythms and phrasing and yet unfailing truthfulness and nail-on-the-head precision. It was about a stripping away of pretense, a peeling away of the excesses that surround sports to find the real truths underneath.

Ineradicable memories seep down inside a person's consciousness and disappear for decades, only to reappear later in the form of ambition—and material. Slowly but surely, my father exerted his influence, a tractor-beam-like pull. I traipsed after him from assignment to assignment, from childhood to adulthood, until his profession became mine. He was from a generation of sportswriters that adopted a demeanor of perpetual nonchalance, cigarettes dangling, so he never talked much about his art or his pride in having a child follow his footsteps. He never said, "Be a writer like me." His instructions were his example: the sound of a typewriter in the back room, which began shortly after I went to bed at night and which was going again when I woke up in the morning. The absoluteness of his concentration, the contrariness of his thinking, and the depth of his respectfulness for good work. All of which together can only be called a kind of integrity.

"Learn your craft," he told me, on one of the few occasions we discussed my future. "And don't ever let a thing go until it's as good as you can make it."

He also said this: "Dad loves his work."

SALLY JENKINS *is an award-winning columnist for* The Washington Post *and the bestselling author of eight books, including* It's Not About the Bike: My Journey Back to Life, *her collaboration with Lance Armstrong;* The Real All Americans, *about Jim Thorpe and the Carlisle Indian Industrial School football squad; and* The State of Jones, *an account of an insurrection in the heart of the Confederacy cowritten with Harvard historian John Stauffer. Jenkins's work has been featured in* GQ *and* Sports Illustrated, *and she has been a correspondent on CNBC as well as on NPR's* All Things Considered. *She lives in New York City.*

When a daughter gets up on a horse, it's often the dad who goes for a ride.

WHOA IS ME

<del>≈≈</del>∿∿<del>≈</del>

Bernie Lincicome

Men will die for ribbons. —NAPOLEON
Dads will max out their credit cards for ribbons.
—HORSE-SHOW FATHER

Dads are suckers for daughters. It only takes one word. Two syllables, maybe three if it is a really big deal.

"Dad-dee."

That will do it. Woe to the man who gets, "Dad-dee ee?"

The consequence of the question stood insolently in his stall. A huge chestnut gelding grinding fodder, *crunch, crunch, crunch,* his large shiny eyes fixing me without welcome.

Here was a literal example of putting on the feed bag,

oats, barley, shredded beet pulp, bran, a little molasses, of which he would require five pounds a day, plus another twenty pounds of hay, maybe ten gallons of water. Did I mention each day?

"When we get him fed up," said Sharon, our daughter's trainer, "he'll be stunning. He's a good first horse."

A chill crept up my neck. There was something ominous in those words. He was already stunning enough for my bank account. But it was the other phrase. First horse. That implied a second, a third horse.

It raised the prospect that this was not going to be a whim, a passage for a young girl between puberty and the prom.

I got through my youth with a single baseball glove, the one I oiled and molded around the baseball, the one I slept with. The left side of my face smelled like neatsfoot oil throughout junior high school. It was not my first glove. It was my glove. It will always be my glove.

My wife, Jaye, a synchronized swimmer, owned two swimsuits as performer, coach, and lifeguard. A good first suit, a good second suit. Not a better suit, just another suit.

It is not a long list, those one-time things—coffins, wedding dresses, toilet paper—but I had no reason to believe a girl's horse would not be somewhere on that list.

This was her horse, my thirteen-year-old daughter's horse, and even after he was fed up, after the hours of training and brushing and bathing, her small hands doing it all, his fate would be to give way to another horse, a better horse.

I considered the name "Already Obsolete" for the show ring. Or maybe "Second Mortgage." I settled on "First Edition."

Lad, the horse's stable name, stood seventeen hands and already weighed an unfed-up 1,200 pounds. The rider, my daughter Romey, stood maybe nine hands—using her hands to measure, not the ordinary five-inch adult hand—and it would be up to her to control this biohazard of bone and muscle and self-interest, making him leap over hurdles, causing him to turn on command, all of this using a piece of wire in his mouth.

They made a good package, I was told, the thin, elegant young girl and the stately beast. Judges like that.

But let's go back to the beginning.

"Dad-dee-ee, could I have a horse?"

Had the question come from my son, David, the answer would have been no, hell, no. He asked for a skateboard, and I gave him a list of chores to complete before he got it.

To my daughter, I said, "You'll need lessons."

Romey spent time at a local suburban pasture near our home, riding bareback on plugs, happily galloping along, laughing with other girls her age. There is something between horses and young girls, as if each looks empty without the other. Studies have been done on the subject.

I could have left her in the pasture, with or without her own horse, happy and with no pressure to please anyone but herself. But fathers want more for their daughters. They want the best for them. And daughters want to please their fathers. It is the way it is.

So I decided to give her a seat. That's the word for it. A hunter seat. She would learn to ride properly, not like a rodeo cowgirl chasing calves—not that there's anything wrong with it—but like a princess. My little princess. She would learn equitation.

Equitation is the highbrow word for when the saddle is the size of a hand towel and has no horn. Sometimes this is known as riding "English."

There is something slippery about that term. You put English on a cue ball to make it do unnatural things. The English muffin is not a muffin at all but a doughy little waffle. You have to take English in school over and over even though you already understand and speak it.

English, indeed. Why not Polish? Or Hungarian? Hunter seat equitation is entirely foreign. Tallyho, riding to hounds. John Wayne did not start the cattle drive by telling Montgomery Clift, "Let's canter them to Montana, Matt."

Sharon, a chain-smoking Michigander, would teach Romey how to ride English. Like any coach, she wanted to see what she had to work with.

Romey climbed upon a rented horse, a benign mare of a certain age that had been through this many times. Walk. Trot. Canter. That's the horse show equivalent of punt, pass, and kick. Around the practice ring they went, at least one of them knowing what she was doing.

"She threw in a flying change," marveled Sharon.

Huh?

Pride in Romey's accomplishment overrode the impulse to ask just what exactly a flying change might be (it might be throwing money at a parking meter or knocking over the tip jar at Starbucks), but to have

Romey throw one in during her first session suggested to me the same feeling Jimmy Evert must have had the first time little Chrissie hit the baseline with two hands on the racket.

The world of sports parenting divides itself into two camps: soccer moms and tennis dads. There is the occasional crossover and the political hybrid, the hockey mom, but I found myself in an entirely new category: the horse-show father.

It is a very small club, and it meets informally outside stables and riding academies. You can find us waiting in our SUVs, fiddling with the radio dial, doing business on our cell phones, or reading box scores about real sports.

Somewhere over there are our daughters, weighing less than a load of wet wash, astride a half-ton animal, making it leap or turn or stop. We have nothing to do with any of it.

A horse-show father does not coach or practice with his child or throw the ball around in the backyard. An HSF is not a participant. He is a banker.

I have played baseball with a bat held together by nails, the baseball without a cover; football with a ball so ground in with grime, it left stains on my hands; basketball with a leaking ball on a dirt court with no net on the rim.

I expected my son to do the same. For my daughter, I made a shopping list.

A good tennis racket (a good first racket) might cost roughly as much as a show jacket. Add a couple cans of balls, find a public court, and the game is on. Golf clubs cost maybe half a saddle.

In show horsing, the list mocks the maker, smirks

toward bankruptcy: helmet, jacket, breeches, boots (custom made for individual calves), boot trees, boot-jack, boot polish, gloves, shirt.

And we have not even come to the horse. Saddle, saddle cloths—one for work, one for show—stirrups, bit, bridle, crop, spurs, girth, reins, brushes, combs, tack box, trailer, trailer hitch, trailer parking lessons . . .

And always the daily feed bill. The worst horse eats as much as the best one. Anyone mucking the stall cannot tell the difference.

Owning a horse is like owning a boat. The difference is that you can park the boat and ignore it, but that animal is going to get his oats and hay whether he is standing or jumping.

The summer show circuit was coming. Pricey lessons on practice horses gave way to the inevitable—actual ownership. To reach her potential, Romey needed a better horse. She favored a cheap, dull little bay with a bit of a sway in his back. Not a good package.

The old thoroughbred trainer Johnny Nerud once fixed the price of horses thus: "A horse is worth fifty dollars and whatever the traffic will bear." The traffic in my case was two months' salary. My root canal was postponed until autumn.

Lad had a Jockey Club registration, had been a flat-track racer and then a steeplechaser. At seven years old, he had traveled down the food chain to show jumper. It seemed to me that his heart was never in it, that somewhere in that pea brain of his was still the roar of the racetrack, the echoes of glory.

The horse-show world is a quiet place, marked by the

occasional pop of a diet-soda can or the crinkling of sandwich cellophane. Crowds do not roar or even become crowds, for that matter. No one ever went to a horse show who did not have a relative in the ring.

Now that Lad was fed up, he could be rank and willful. Not every rider could keep him on the right lead, take him into a jump at the right spot, override his urges with her will. And Romey had bruises to prove it. More than once she was deposited into a manure pile. I did not find it remarkable that she kept getting back on the horse.

Equestrian sports rank somewhere next to quoits in the public awareness. A promotion in the United Kingdom (yes, English again) aimed to get a greater horse-show audience by having young women ride in tight T-shirts, white briefs, and boots. Hooters on a horse.

The gimmick met with mixed success. While the reduced wardrobe might appeal to the checkbook, we horse-show fathers are like all fathers: We are for more clothing on our daughters, not less.

We tell ourselves the sport is healthy and satisfying. When a ninety-pound child can make a half-ton horse do whatever she wants it to do, the confidence gained is immeasurable.

We take note that the lessons of sports are there to be learned, as from any other sport. Such as discipline, for instance. A seven-year-old girl is trying to canter her pony in the practice ring before a show. The trainer yells at her to get the pony on the right lead. She fails.

"If you don't get this right," the trainer yells, "I'm going to make you do five laps without stirrups."

We believe the sport builds character. A judge has placed a girl third who feels she should have been first. "What's this crud?" she demands of the judge. "Are you blind or taking lessons in stupidity?"

John McEnroe, eat your heart out.

In baseball they yell, "Kill the umpire." Horse-show fathers are not so crude. We are content to just put him out of work for a couple of days.

The sport is not without scandal. There are periodic reports of doping of horses—not to make them faster, as on a racetrack, but to make them less hyper, a disadvantage for either show or sale.

But most impressively and importantly, the sport involves the father in his daughter's activity. At my daughter's first show, the ring was muddy and a young girl's horse balked at a jump, tossing her over its head toward the slop.

"Save the coat!" yelled her dad.

The girl broke her fall with her rump instead of with her elbows. A bruise is nothing compared to ruining a $400 show jacket.

The announcement came from a portable PA system. "Now up, rider number seventeen, Romey Lincicome on First Edition."

I could see across the show ring my little girl sitting calmly and confidently on her horse, Lad's mane braided and his tail shining and untangled from a fresh brushing.

Romey gauged the course layout, punching the air with her gloved finger as she counted out the jumps. Some invisible signal, from her legs, from her seat, from somewhere in all those hours of practice, started the horse on his way at an instant trot.

Over the first rail, straight to the lattice gate, turn to the picket fence, another rail, up over the geraniums, turn again and back, the combination, the water, the double rail. Halt. Smile. Applause.

How had this happened? Where in all those days and hours of trotting and cantering and washing and brushing and mucking, while I was nose-deep in box scores, just a waiting taxi, had this child become this performer, this athlete?

I had to admit my expectations were low. I had treated the whole thing as an indulgence. I even took a bit of pleasure in being able to nag about the expense. Now all I could do was blush from pride.

There it was. The first show, the first ribbon hanging from the bridle of the first horse.

"Thanks, Dad," Romey said, walking the huge red animal past me from the show ring.

Dad. One syllable. How economical. How grown up.

BERNIE LINCICOME *does not regret spending his life writing about sports. Nor does he take the blame for the death of his last newspaper, the* Rocky Mountain News. *He wishes to point out that for the seventeen years he wrote the "In the Wake of the News" sports column for the* Chicago Tribune, *both he and the paper were in perfect health. Bernie is still doing fine.*

*Time was when a tennis pro couldn't get any respect.
In this case, not even from his five-year-old daughter.
But little did the young Chris Evert realize that her father
was about to create a masterpiece.*

THE FAMILY BUSINESS

—⌇⌇—

Chris Evert with Jon Levey

When I was five years old, I was on a popular children's program in South Florida called *The Skipper Chuck Show.* The small studio audience was all kids, and there was a segment in which Skipper Chuck would ask them questions. It just so happened that on my lone appearance, the Skip put a microphone in front of me and asked my name and what my dad did for a living. I had no hesitation telling him my name was Chris Evert. I pulled up short, however, before revealing my father's occupation. My dad was a tennis coach, and fifty years ago *nobody's* dad was a tennis coach. Childhood insecurity and embarrassment got the better of me, and I gave my dad what I felt was a more reputable line of work.

"He's a painter," I said.

Obviously my attraction to tennis—and my respect for those who teach the game—was not immediate. In fact, early on I was resentful at being forced into playing. When I was in kindergarten, each day after school I would go to my best friend's house to swim and eat barbecue for dinner. Nothing in life could compare. It was about that time my father decided he was going to teach me how to play tennis. Instead of going to my friend's house, he took me to the tennis facility in Holiday Park in Fort Lauderdale, where he was the head pro. We'd go onto the court with a shopping cart full of balls and he'd toss them to me endlessly, drilling into me the fundamentals. In terms of fun, it was nothing to write home about—certainly not on a par with a swim in a pool and a grilled burger.

But tennis was in Jimmy Evert's blood. A child of the Great Depression, my dad was exposed to the sport as a ball boy for Bill Tilden. He honed his skills on courts made of wooden boards in his native Chicago. He received a tennis scholarship to Notre Dame, where he was captain and played No. 1 singles. After graduating, he had some success on the men's tour, winning the Canadian Open and the U.S. Indoors. But after serving in the Navy, my dad wanted a steady income and decided that, rather than competing, he would teach tennis. His first job was at a club in New Rochelle, New York, where he met my mom, Colette. Before long, he was spending winters down in Florida, teaching at Holiday Park. Soon it became their permanent home.

While some tennis pros are reluctant to coach their

kids, my dad never hesitated to teach his children the game. He started all five of us when each was six years old, and all five took to the sport and made it a significant part of our lives. A major reason for that was the atmosphere my dad created at Holiday Park. Before Nick Bollettieri opened his academy farther north, Holiday Park was the mecca of tennis in Florida. One year we had more than ten players training there to compete at Wimbledon. Future Top 10 men's players Brian Gottfried and Harold Solomon were regulars and took lessons from my dad. Many years later, Jennifer Capriati would too. Best of all, Holiday Park was a public facility.

There were dozens of talented players my age there, which afforded me tough competition and a social life. When I woke in the morning, I couldn't wait to hit the courts—to work on my game, of course, but also to clown with my friends and family. I remember one summer, we painted lines on a patch of grass and tied a net around two trees to construct our own grass court. Perhaps I didn't have a choice whether or not to play tennis, but it did turn out to be an idyllic childhood.

That's not to say my dad was a soft coach; his tireless work ethic set such an example. Each day he was on the court for nearly twelve hours without a break. He and I spent countless hours on the clay courts perfecting my footwork, strokes, and patience. I was small and not the type of player who was going to pile up winners, so my dad built my game around minimizing errors. The idea was that my opponents would falter before I would. It called for endless drilling and repetition, which was tough on me because I didn't always love to practice. Most players—even those known for their icy demeanors, like Bjorn Borg and Roger Federer—were emotional on the court as juniors. I was no different. I threw and broke my share of rackets. But my dad taught me something that became instrumental to my success: how to bottle my emotions during a match and never give my opponents an indication of how I was feeling. Even if I was losing or felt exhausted, I shouldn't show it. Playing with a poker face would frustrate my opponents into making mistakes. Consequently, that was the way I conducted my career.

It proved to be a genius tactic. I always felt confident that if a match was close, I would have the mental edge. It was probably my greatest strength. Would I have preferred to play with more emotion? Sure. Giving full effort and winning are always appreciated, but I think fans relate more easily to athletes who wear their hearts on their sleeves. It wasn't that my father didn't want me to play in an engaging style. I doubt the concept of showmanship even entered his mind. He just did what a good coach is supposed to: He gave me the best possible chance to win.

And he never once got mad when I lost a match; he never yelled or put pressure on me to excel. As long as I tried my best, my dad was satisfied. He wasn't driven to nurture a Grand Slam champion or fulfill his own career dreams. When I was in eighth grade, I was competing in tournaments two weekends a month and doing quite well. At the same time, I wanted to feel like just another one of the girls at school. So without really thinking about it, I tried out and made the boys' basketball cheer-leading squad. It would have been a significant time commitment that interfered with tennis. My dad told me I had a decision to make. He wasn't going to give me his full support and spend all his free time with me on the tennis court if what I wanted was to become a cheer-leader. I thought about it, and in the end it was a fairly obvious choice to make. Still, that was a defining mo-ment for me, because I realized I would have to make sacrifices in order to reach my potential. And I have al-ways respected my dad for allowing me to come to that conclusion on my own.

Inevitably, though, there were times when he blurred the line between coach and father. At night, after we had spent the entire day on the court, he would occasionally still have tennis on the brain. He'd want to discuss a stroke I was trying to refine or the match from earlier that day. I was in my early teens, and I needed more emotional and less athletic support from him. I needed him to tell me I looked pretty that day or to say he was proud of me.

"Oh, Chrissie, he never had sisters," my mom would say, trying to defend my dad's lack of sensitivity.

His was a generation of tight lips—compliments weren't handed out liberally. My drive to succeed in ten-nis was probably partly due to a desire to get praise from my dad. When I entered my late teens and had been on tour for a few years, we made more of an effort to address our relationship. I needed him to be more of a dad, and he was fully supportive of my getting a traveling coach to lessen his role. That took the pressure off him and allowed him to enjoy just being a parent. When I was on the road, I would call home every night and I would talk with him about whatever tournament I was playing in. His was the voice I wanted to hear after I suffered a tough loss—he always found a way to soothe me and point out the positives.

Over the course of my career, we did most of our communicating over the phone. He didn't go to many pro tournaments because he has a hard time being in large crowds and can suffer from agoraphobia. He was there for only one of my U.S. Open titles and never saw me win Wimbledon or the French Open. Of course, I wanted him to be there, but overall his absence didn't bother me too much. He got anxious in those types of situations, and it would have worried me knowing he was uncomfortable.

That's why my mom was the perfect complement. Besides being an extrovert and a born traveler, she served as the equalizer between us. My dad frowned on dates and thought that going out late on weekends would hurt my game. My mom believed all work and no play made for an unhappy person. She made sure all my brothers and sisters had balance in their lives. Yet she was devoted to our tennis as much as my father was, taking us all over Florida to play in different tournaments. My parents gave up their weekends and never went on a vacation. A favorite family trip was when we all piled into the family station wagon, complete with a bed in the back, and headed to the USTA National Open (for girls under twelve) in Chattanooga, Tennessee. In a sport that's notorious for bringing out the worst in parents, I couldn't have been luckier.

Thanks to our dad's passion, tennis was truly a family pastime. All the Evert kids won a national junior tournament at some point. My younger sister, Jeanne, went pro as I did and made it into the Top 20 early on in her career. My other siblings all got college scholarships and played No. 1 singles for their schools. To this day, my dad says he's just as proud of them as he is of me. They worked hard, too, and he's thrilled he never had to pay a dime for college.

His beneficiaries aren't all named Evert either. It would be impossible to count the number of players who spent time on my father's court. Whether they were looking for a college scholarship or a reliable backhand volley, my dad was there to see they achieved their goals. After he retired in 1997, the tennis facility at Holiday Park was renamed the Jimmy Evert Tennis Center. It was a great honor for him but completely deserved. No one has had a bigger impact on the success and popularity of tennis in Southern Florida than my dad. He certainly made all the difference in my career.

Not bad for a painter.

CHRIS EVERT *was ranked No. 1 in the world for 260 weeks and won eighteen Grand Slam singles titles. She currently runs a tennis academy in Boca Raton, Florida, where she lives with her three sons, Alex, Nicky, and Colton.*

She may not remember her first NBA game, but her father, the Sports Guy, will never forget.

TWINKLE, TWINKLE, LITTLE STAR

≈≈≈≈

Bill Simmons

I love fatherhood for the little things. Like having the power to derail any tantrum with five simple words: "Wanna get some ice cream?" Like stepping in on those last few bites of grilled cheese, because kids never finish a meal. Like being awakened each morning by a smiling kid instead of a blaring alarm clock. Like having my own mini-McMahon who laughs at every joke I make, especially if it involves flatulence.

As the old saying goes, children make us appreciate what we stopped appreciating long ago. (I don't know who said it, but it's been said. And if it hasn't been said, then please, let me say it.) Ever wonder why Larry King sired two more after turning 125 years old? Because he's selfish, that's why. He wanted those last chances to appreciate the little things.

I totally get that. In the past few weeks, I've relived the following experiences through the eyes of my two-and-a-half-year-old daughter: the joyous celebration after the Sox won the World Series (she loved watching everyone jump on each other); trick-or-treating; a first trip to the movies (she threw an impressive complete game at *Bee Movie*); and, finally, a first real live NBA game (Cavaliers at Clippers).

I most wanted to see her reaction to the game. She has actually liked hoops ever since it became part of her nighttime routine last spring. As far as she knew, our TVs could show only Red Sox games and NBA playoff games after six p.m. (See, I told you kids are great! They'll believe anything!) She gravitated toward basketball because of its colors and sounds, the running and jumping, the tattoos and chest-thumping and, most of all, the simplicity. Basically, players try to make the basketball rip through the net, and when they do, everyone applauds.

Now, here's where my demented genius comes in: I think that kids can be brainwashed to believe anything is fun as long as you seem excited about it. You could say to your child right now, "You know what we're doing later? We're heading to the yard to watch grass grow!" And if you sell it well enough, they'll be counting the minutes until the back door opens. Seriously. So when I asked my half-asleep daughter if she wanted to watch basketball in Daddy's bed, I made it sound more fun than mashing bananas with The Wiggles. In retrospect, I probably didn't need to sell it so hard. She was so happy to get called up to the majors (Mommy and Daddy's bed) and maybe get her head rubbed too. But that's how she was introduced to basketball: I brainwashed her, lied to her, and wore her down.

Fast-forward to the November 11 [2007] Cavs–Clips game. When I asked if she wanted to go, I presented the offer as if I were suggesting we fly in a helicopter to eat M&Ms on the moon. And I sold LeBron as a combination of Santa, Elmo, and our UPS guy. After a few YouTube clips, she was hooked, screaming at her mom, "We're gonna go see LeBron!" Her excitement only amplified over the next few days. Meanwhile, I started to worry, because 150 minutes is a long time to keep a child entertained. Could she make it through the third quarter? Could she even make it to halftime? Would she melt down like Fausto Carmona at Fenway?

As soon as we got inside the Staples Center, I immediately bought a bucket of popcorn that was bigger than Eddy Curry. (We learned at *Bee Movie* that a big bucket buys you thirty-five solid minutes, even if it might cause diarrhea later. Whatever.) We missed the national anthem but caught the pregame intros; she was transfixed when the arena went dark. We found our seats in time for the opening tip, and within about 3.2 seconds, she was on my lap and promptly entering "The ADD Zone," an inevitability for any little kid who is digesting too many images and noises at once. The Zone-Out—and the Art Shell Face that accompanies it—lasted for a good ten minutes, just her staring straight ahead as she shoveled popcorn into her mouth. It was like the Raiders' 2006 team video.

She eventually emerged from her stupor and started to ask about the JumboTron, which she mistook for a giant TV. Could we touch it? (Um, no.) Was there a remote control? (Sadly, no.) After the fifty-seventh straight JumboTron-related question, I steered her toward LeBron. She was captivated as she watched him lope around, right up until she became distracted by the referees' whistles (she wanted one for herself), the substitution horn (she liked the way it sounded), and everyone who was eating and drinking around us ("Look, he has popcorn too").

She liked how the players huddled in a circle for time-outs, as well as my revelation that the players had their own "teacher" (the coach). She liked putting her drink in the cupholder that comes with each seat. In fact, she liked it so much she must have done it 735 times in twenty minutes. She was so delighted by the Clippers dancers that I'm more worried than ever about keeping her off the pole (every father's most important job). She loved clapping with the crowd after each Clippers basket, and she loved hearing the crowd boo and yell after a dubious nontraveling call on LeBron. And she got a special kick out of the guy behind us calling one of the referees a jackass. Really, she loved it all.

But two moments stand out above the rest. In the second quarter, LeBron swiped a pass and had a clear path right in front of us to a breakaway dunk. I nudged her eagerly—watch this, watch this!—as the crowd started buzzing and flashbulbs went off. When Bron-Bron delivered the goods with a hellacious double-clutch jam, everyone was delighted, including my daughter, who screamed out loud and giggled afterward. (She officially loves LeBron now. At least, I think she does. She kept getting him confused with Larry Hughes and Daniel Gibson.)

The other moment occurred when the crowd improbably broke out the wave, quite possibly the single greatest moment of her young life. She loved watching it slowly ripple around the stadium, waiting for it to reach our section and then jumping up with her arms raised to yell at the top of her lungs. To be honest, I've always thought the wave was reprehensible. But not anymore. Anything that makes my kid that happy is fine with me.

Unfortunately, she threw only seven innings because of a Grady Little–level managerial mistake on my part: At halftime, we shared a large Sprite and one of those pretzels covered with cinnamon and sugar. I may as well have administered an eight ball. What was I thinking? By the end of the third quarter, after she'd turned into the Great Cornholio and started to sing "Twinkle, Twinkle, Little Star" at the top of her lungs, I knew we had to leave before she kicked a hole through the seat of the poor guy in front of us.

The good news: She threw a tantrum; she wanted to stay. I guess if I'd had a moment to reflect as I hauled my wailing child out of the Staples Center, I'd have realized the NBA had itself another fan. Instead, I had to stop the commotion: "Wanna get some ice cream?"

BILL SIMMONS, *who writes the "Sports Guy" column for ESPN.com, is the author of the national bestseller* The Book of Basketball, *an executive producer for ESPN's* 30 for 30 *documentary project, and the father of two.*

*The following essay was written in 2007 when the author,
the daughter of David Hirshey, a longtime book editor
and soccer writer (coauthor of* The ESPN World Cup
Companion)*, was applying to Dartmouth. She got in.*

TO WHOM IT MAY CONCERN

⌐∿∾⌐

Emily Hirshey

"Some people think football is a matter of life and death. I don't like
that attitude. I can assure them it is much more serious than that."
—BILL SHANKLY, FORMER LIVERPOOL MANAGER

My father is obsessed with soccer. No. Let me
rephrase that. My father lives for soccer. It's his
passion, his *raison d'être*. For my mother, soccer is
the other woman. For me, an only child, soccer is my
attention-hogging sibling. Not to say he isn't a loving
husband and father, but my mother and I never seemed
to stand a chance in the war for my dad's undying
affection.

When a pregnant woman announces her baby is kicking, her husband is supposed to express excitement and
joy. With my father, it was paranoia: "Is she kicking

with the laces or her toe?" "Does it feel like a forward or a defender?" While other kids were learning to walk, I was dribbling; while most little girls have nicknames like "Princess," my father insisted on calling me "Crusher." I swear I came out of the womb wearing shin guards.

As a child, I completely adored my father and every minute we spent together, albeit that time was devoted either to drills in Central Park or cheering on the MetroStars at Giants Stadium. But I didn't care what we were doing, as long as I remained "Daddy's little goal-scoring girl." Only later did it occur to me that these were the only minutes we spent together.

I was five when my father signed me up for little league soccer, and, of course, he was the coach of my first team. (And every subsequent team until high school.) Those first years in little league remain the most fun I've ever had playing, because it wasn't about becoming the next Mia Hamm; it was about having fun. Though I continued on to a travel team, the purity of soccer was tarnished for me once it became competitive. Inevitably, there was a backlash.

By tenth grade, our mutual passion had become the bane of my existence. At that point, I knew soccer would never be the air I breathe, my driving force. I started faking illness to avoid practice and prayed to be put on the bench during games. I fought endlessly with my father about this newfound apathy toward our once mutual fixation. Our conflict over soccer divided my household and even (as my mother recently admitted) threatened my parents' marriage. There were many nights I stayed up crying—sure that if I stopped playing, my father would never love me the way he had once loved his Crusher. On the field, whenever an opposing player scored a goal, I saw it as a point of adoration I had lost from my father. His greatest joy was now my deepest misery, and I couldn't sacrifice my happiness for his. I quit.

For months following this fateful decision, Dad and I barely spoke and we hugged only when a picture was being taken. I was terrified that things would never be the same—that soccer had been our only bond, and now I had broken it. Meanwhile, he continued coaching, and whenever he raved about one of his players, I was positive that he'd prefer her as a daughter. When I accused him of this, I saw the heartbreak in his eyes, but I was set on convincing myself that it was true. It was my way of punishing myself for not living up to his expectations. My self-loathing, masked as disdain for my father, only deepened our rift. It was my fault. I had let my fear of losing him shroud any love of the game I'd ever possessed.

I realize now that the truth is that, saccharine though it may sound, my father only ever wanted me to love soccer because to love soccer was to love him, and, all the while, I assumed that he would only love me if I loved soccer. But slowly, by some inexplicable force, I began to see that my thinking was flawed. It took a while, but there came a time when once again I found myself beaming when I heard the familiar sound of Fox Soccer Channel blaring from my parents' bedroom.

A few years ago, my father and I renewed an old

connection and began going to Knicks games. I was only three years old when Dad and I paid the first of our sporadic visits to Madison Square Garden together, but now it turned into a routine. This bond, at least, could remain pure and lasting, so we held on to it as tight as we could, as soccer no longer united us. Now, every October, there comes the day when my father announces who we're going to see play at Madison Square Garden that season, and it is at this moment when I see how important our friendship is to him, how maintaining a connection is as important to him as it is to me. There is no day in the year more meaningful to me than this one.

This past July, when Zinedine Zidane was given that red card during the final game of the World Cup, my father and I both stared at the TV, weeping. He was crying for the love of the game, while I was crying for the love of my father, who I now knew would love me just as much if my eyes were dry.

Emily Hirshey is a student at Dartmouth College, where she is a staff writer for the student paper, The Dartmouth.

A former big-league pitcher assumed that having a daughter meant that nobody would follow in his footsteps to the pitcher's mound. Then she threw him a curve.

DEAR ABBY

—∿∿∿—

Bob Tufts

I always wanted to have a daughter.

I remembered how much trouble my brother and I had caused our parents compared to our sister, Sandy. Raising a daughter would be so much easier than raising a boy, it seemed to me. (Those of you with teenage girls in your family can stop laughing anytime.) Especially with regard to sports. I didn't want to have a son who somehow felt that he must follow in my footsteps—I pitched (albeit briefly) in the major leagues for the San Francisco Giants and Kansas City Royals—to play baseball. I wouldn't have wanted other people dissecting his athletic ability and comparing him to me on every play.

After all, I had had enough trouble following in the foot-steps of my brother, Bill, who was an all-state pitcher and received a baseball scholarship to the University of Florida.

When my daughter, Abby, was born nearly twenty years ago, I thought to myself that we would share base-ball as fans, without the pressure a boy would have felt to make the travel team or play at the highest level of his age group. I could share my love of baseball with Abby, telling her stories of games, people, and places, and all the while she could blaze her own trail in every aspect of life, including sports (if desired), to her own satisfaction. Her life, her choices—I would merely support whatever she decided to do.

However, I did wind up using undue parental influ-ence and authority when it came to her being a baseball fan. From birth, Abby was not-so-subtly reminded by me that baseball was the preeminent American game—at least in our home. When she was just two months old, Abby "experienced" her first contact with the game. I decided that my first Father's Day present would be to spend the afternoon alone with my daughter watching a Mets–Phillies game on TV. My wife, Suzanne, and her mother, Henriette, went out to lunch at the Boathouse in Central Park. Abby had her bottle and bounced back and forth in her comfy chair while I sat in an overstuffed lounge chair with my sandwich and beverage. We both fell asleep long before the game ended on a ninth-inning home run by Von Hayes off Randy Myers.

Abby was always allowed to watch a few innings of ball games at night before going to bed. When it became time to try to properly indoctrinate Abby, I decided that she should root for the Yankees. This was a sort of compromise, as I grew up a Red Sox fan and Suzanne liked the Mets. I wasn't going to make a poor New York City kid support Boston, and considering how the Mets performed during the early nineties, the Yankees were clearly the best choice. Looking back on their imminent dynasty, the timing couldn't have been better, and Buck Showalter's controlling managerial style meant that Abby might pick up subtle facets of the game by seeing the Yanks play.

The first thing she learned was the batting order. One night while we were watching a Yankees–Mariners game, the phone rang, and I left the room for a few minutes. When I came back, Abby asked if she could stay up until Ken Griffey, Jr., batted for the Mariners. (She had become a Griffey and Randy Johnson fan thanks to the 1994 movie *Little Big League*.) Without thinking, I agreed to her supposedly innocent request. Little did I realize that Griffey had made the last out of the previous inning while I was out of the room. Abby's clever lineup maneuver bought her about an extra hour before bedtime.

She attended her first game at Shea when she was seven years old. We left after six innings due to the plodding action on the field and the fact that she had tried all six food concession items. But it was fun explaining in a calm parent voice why Mets catcher Todd Hundley was screaming at the Cubs pitcher who had just knocked him down on an 0–2 pitch and how, when the pitcher came up to bat the next inning, the Mets pitcher would probably knock him down, and then everyone would get mad and run out of the dugouts and bullpens to scream at one another. When the retaliation and resulting histrionics occurred much as I predicted, she thought I was the most brilliant person on the face of the earth.

Over the years, Abby met former players like Goose Gossage, Bob Feller, and Frank Robinson through my charity work with the Major League Baseball Players Alumni Association. She got strange looks from Bill Lee and Barney Schultz when she talked to them while wearing her Yankees jacket, so I had to explain to her the history of the Boston animosity to pinstripes. She also met and talked to women athletes like Billie Jean King, who told Abby that when I was called up to the majors by the San Francisco Giants, I replaced King's brother, Randy Moffitt, on the roster.

Abby played some youth sports as a preteen but didn't care for most of them. Per my original inclination, I let her find her own favorite game. Soccer and basketball bored her, as did most traditional sports. She tried Thai boxing at summer camp and was pretty good at it. Abby had to fight one of the boys in the final, as no girl could compete with her. She was giving the young lad a good beating, which he stopped by punching her in the nose, which caused his disqualification. But to her credit, Abby realized that beating up boys is a poor sports career choice for a young girl.

She enjoyed competition, but no sport truly excited her until she discovered volleyball in middle school. Unfortunately, her passion wasn't shared by a lot of the other girls at school—many of them the daughters of diplomats and foreign-born executives, who viewed girls' sports differently than Americans do—and Abby's first athletic love almost died a premature death for lack of interest. She took the initiative, begging, coaxing, and pleading with her friends and begging, coaxing, and pleading with the coaches in order to assemble a team, and she succeeded.

Once she got past that organizational hurdle, she began to excel at a sport of which I had limited knowledge. I now became a spectator—with full vested interest in a game for the first time since I stopped playing baseball professionally in 1983—and I was enthralled. Abby developed a powerful serve and quickly became the best player on her team, despite her young age. She also developed true sportsmanship, signaling "I'm sorry" in sign language to a player from a school for the deaf after hitting her in the head with a kill.

When she moved on to boarding school, her sports schedule became an important part of our family life. We took beautiful drives in all seasons to the Berkshire School in Sheffield, Massachusetts, to see regattas, softball games, and volleyball matches, all followed by dinners in Great Barrington and talks about the teams and her classes. Abby was now sharing her sports life with me as I had shared my baseball life with her. But this time I was the one being educated by my daughter.

I realized that rowing was not Abby's favorite sport when she said, "I don't know what to do with crew. I don't see myself spending my life as a galley slave." In fact, the main reason she liked it was that "you really feel great once you stop rowing."

It was more fun watching her play softball. She played outfield with reckless abandon. Once, while playing left field, she dove headfirst for a sinking liner, caught the ball, and planted her face deep into the out-field grass. She sat up, held the ball up, teetered, and slumped over. The dizziness soon faded. After the game, the first thing she said was, "Did you see me hold it up? No way was I going to let the umpire call it a hit." Abby also pitched, and I chuckled at the thought of my daughter on the mound, considering my worries about a son following in my footsteps. I was more nervous watching her pitch than I was when I played!

Abby had a propensity for playing well on her birthday. She drove in the winning run with a single to beat Miss Hall's during her sophomore year. Unfortunately, I only heard the crack of the bat, as I was getting pizzas out of the car for Abby and the team when it happened.

Volleyball was Abby's most serious sport, and she showed a level of intensity and dedication that I had never seen in her. She was able to visualize the upcoming play as it developed. She learned (certainly without any help from me) how to play every position on the court as well as possible. She played every minute of every match her sophomore and junior years, except for one game missed due to injury. She was co-captain her junior and senior years and was a three-time league All-Star.

The Berkshire team was a very good squad during her three years on the varsity, making the New England playoffs each season. Getting there wasn't always easy. Sophomore year, Berkshire needed to win a home game against the Westover School—which was in first place and had beaten Berkshire badly early in the season—and the next game to make the playoffs.

Unlike me during my career, Abby wasn't nervous about playing in front of her parents and encouraged our involvement. Abby called us the night before the Westover match and told us that she wanted us to be vocal the next afternoon. She wanted to hear us and feed off the fans' energy. I was a little reluctant at first, for fear that I would be marked as a lunatic parent, but I complied. Just before the fourth game of the match, with Berkshire leading 2–1, I shouted extra loud, "Not in our house!" Abby was resting on the bench with her hands on her knees. She picked up her head, turned to me with a huge smile, and nodded with a wink. They won the fourth set easily to win that contest, took the next match as well, and qualified for the New England playoffs.

Abby is now in her second year at Dickinson College in Pennsylvania, and despite her love of volleyball, she recently decided to stop playing in order to concentrate on a career in sports management. She's using the time she spent on practices and year-round training to work for the school's athletic director and sports-information director as well as the swimming and baseball teams.

I'm glad I had a daughter who shares my love of sports, who shaped her own athletic identity, and who has embarked on her own journey in the sports world. I'm also glad that she generously shared her sports life with me. As I said before: Her life, her choices—and I proudly support her in whatever she decides to do next.

BOB TUFTS *is a former major league relief pitcher with the San Francisco Giants and Kansas City Royals. He lives in Forest Hills, New York.*

*Even beyond the context of the ballpark, the phrase
"keeping score" calls up notions of accountability and
fairness—the sort of themes that would appeal to a young girl
destined to become a Pulitzer Prize–winning historian.*

KEEPING SCORE

⸺⌇⌇⌇⸺

Doris Kearns Goodwin

When I was six, my father gave me a bright-red
scorebook that opened my heart to the game of
baseball. After dinner on long summer nights, he would
sit beside me in our small enclosed porch to hear my account of that day's Brooklyn Dodger game. Night after
night he taught me the odd collection of symbols, numbers, and letters that enable a baseball lover to record
every action of the game. Our score sheets had blank
boxes in which we could draw our own slanted lines
in the form of a diamond as we followed players around
the bases. Wherever the baserunner's progress stopped,
the line stopped. He instructed me to fill in the unused

boxes at the end of each inning with an elaborate checkerboard design which made it absolutely clear who had been the last to bat and who would lead off the next inning. By the time I had mastered the art of scorekeeping, a lasting bond had been forged among my father, baseball, and me.

All through the summer of 1949, my first summer as a fan, I spent my afternoons sitting cross-legged before the squat Philco radio which stood as a permanent fixture on our porch in Rockville Centre, on the South Shore of Long Island, New York. With my scorebook spread before me, I attended games through the courtly voice of Dodger announcer Red Barber. As he announced the lineup, I carefully printed each player's name in a column on the left side of my sheet. Then, using the standard system my father had taught me, which assigned a number to each position in the field, starting with a "1" for the pitcher and ending with a "9" for the rightfielder, I recorded every play. I found it difficult at times to sit still. As the Dodgers came to bat, I would walk around the room, talking to the players as if they were standing in front of me. At critical junctures, I tried to make a bargain, whispering and cajoling while Pee Wee Reese or Duke Snider stepped into the batter's box: "Please, please, get a hit. If you get a hit now, I'll make my bed every day for a week." Sometimes, when the score was close and the opposing team at bat with men on base, I was too agitated to listen. Asking my mother to keep notes, I left the house for a walk around the block, hoping that when I returned the enemy threat would be over, and once again we'd be up at bat. Mostly, however,

I stayed at my post, diligently recording each inning so that, when my father returned from his job as bank examiner for the state of New York, I could re-create for him the game he had missed.

When my father came home from the city, he would change from his three-piece suit into long pants and a short-sleeved sport shirt, and come downstairs for the ritual Manhattan cocktail with my mother. Then my parents would summon me for dinner from my play on the street outside our house. All through dinner I had to restrain myself from telling him about the day's game, waiting for the special time to come when we would sit together on the couch, my scorebook on my lap.

"Well, did anything interesting happen today?" he would begin. And even before the daily question was completed I had eagerly launched into my narrative of every play, and almost every pitch, of that afternoon's contest. It never crossed my mind to wonder if, at the close of a day's work, he might find my lengthy account the least bit tedious. For there was mastery as well as pleasure in our nightly ritual. Through my knowledge, I commanded my father's undivided attention, the sign of his love. It would instill in me an early awareness of the power of narrative, which would introduce a lifetime of storytelling, fueled by the naive confidence that others would find me as entertaining as my father did.

Michael Francis Aloysius Kearns, my father, was a short man who appeared much larger on account of his erect bearing, broad chest, and thick neck. He had a ruddy Irish complexion, and his green eyes flashed with humor and vitality. When he smiled his entire face was transformed, radiating enthusiasm and friendliness. He called me "Bubbles," a pet name he had chosen, he told me, because I seemed to enjoy so many things. Anxious to confirm his description, I refused to let my enthusiasm wane, even when I grew tired or grumpy. Thus excitement about things became a habit, a part of my personality, and the expectation that I should enjoy new experiences often engendered the enjoyment itself.

These nightly recountings of the Dodgers' progress provided my first lessons in the narrative art. From the scorebook, with its tight squares of neatly arranged symbols, I could unfold the tale of an entire game and tell a story that seemed to last almost as long as the game itself. At first, I was unable to resist the temptation to skip ahead to an important play in later innings. At times, I grew so excited about a Dodger victory that I blurted out the final score before I had hardly begun. But as I became more experienced in my storytelling, I learned to build a dramatic story with a beginning, middle, and end. Slowly, I learned that if I could recount the game, one batter at a time, inning by inning, without divulging the outcome, I could keep the suspense and my father's interest alive until the very last pitch. Sometimes I pretended that I was the great Red Barber himself, allowing my voice to swell when reporting a home run, quieting to a whisper when the action grew tense, injecting tidbits about the players into my reports. At critical moments, I would jump from the couch to illustrate a ball that turned foul at the last moment or a dropped fly that was scored as an error.

"How many hits did Roy Campanella get?" my dad

would ask. Tracing my finger across the horizontal line that represented Campanella's at bats that day, I would count. "One, two, three. Three hits, a single, a double, and another single." "How many strikeouts for Don Newcombe?" It was easy. I would count the Ks. "One, two . . . eight. He had eight strikeouts." Then he'd ask me more subtle questions about different plays—whether a strikeout was called or swinging, whether the double play was around the horn, whether the single that won the game was hit to left or right. If I had scored carefully, using the elaborate system he had taught me, I would know the answers. My father pointed to the second inning, where Jackie Robinson had hit a single and then stolen second. There was excitement in his voice. "See, it's all here. While Robinson was dancing off second, he rattled the pitcher so badly that the next two guys walked to load the bases. That's the impact Robinson makes, game after game. Isn't he something?" His smile at such moments inspired me to take my responsibility seriously.

Sometimes, a particular play would trigger in my father a memory of a similar situation in a game when he was young, and he would tell me stories about the Dodgers when he was a boy growing up in Brooklyn. His vivid tales featured strange heroes such as Casey Stengel, Zack Wheat, and Jimmy Johnston. Though it was hard at first to imagine that the Casey Stengel I knew, the manager of the Yankees, with his colorful language and hilarious antics, was the same man as the Dodger outfielder who hit an inside-the-park home run at the first game ever played at Ebbets Field, my father so skillfully stitched together the past and the present that I felt as if I were living in different time zones. If I closed my eyes, I imagined I was at Ebbets Field in the 1920s for that celebrated game when Dodger right-fielder Babe Herman hit a double with the bases loaded, and, through a series of mishaps on the base paths, three Dodgers ended up at third base at the same time. And I was sitting by my father's side, five years before I was born, when the lights were turned on for the first time at Ebbets Field, the crowd gasping and then cheering as the summer night was transformed into startling day.

When I had finished describing the game, it was time to go to bed, unless I could convince my father to tally each player's batting average, reconfiguring his statistics to reflect the developments of that day's game. If Reese went 3 for 5 and had started the day at .303, my father showed me, by adding and multiplying all the numbers in his head, that his average would rise to .305. If Snider went 0 for 4 and started the day at .301, then his average would dip four points below the .300 mark. If Carl Erskine had let in three runs in seven innings, then my father would multiply three times nine, divide that by the number of innings pitched, and magically tell me whether Erskine's earned-run average had improved or worsened. It was this facility with numbers that had made it possible for my father to pass the civil-service test and become a bank examiner despite leaving school after the eighth grade. And this job had carried him from a Brooklyn tenement to a house with a lawn on Southard Avenue in Rockville Centre.

All through that summer, my father kept from me the

knowledge that running box scores appeared in the daily newspapers. He never mentioned that these abbreviated histories had been a staple feature of the sports pages since the nineteenth century and were generally the first thing he and his fellow commuters turned to when they opened the *Daily News* and the *Herald Tribune* in the morning. I believed that, if I did not recount the games he had missed, my father would never have been able to follow our Dodgers the proper way, day by day, play by play, inning by inning. In other words, without me, his love of baseball would be forever unfulfilled.

DORIS KEARNS GOODWIN *won the Pulitzer Prize in history for her book about Franklin and Eleanor Roosevelt,* No Ordinary Time, *and is the bestselling author of* Wait Till Next Year; Lyndon Johnson and the American Dream; The Fitzgeralds and the Kennedys; *and, most recently,* Team of Rivals: The Political Genius of Abraham Lincoln, *which is often cited as one of President Obama's favorite books. Goodwin, who has made many television appearances as a political analyst, was the first female journalist allowed into the Boston Red Sox locker room. She lives in Concord, Massachusetts, with her husband, Richard Goodwin.*

*What's in a name? Just ask the author's
soccer-crazy daughters.*

ARSENAL GIRLS

~~∞∿~~

Steve Rushin

Sometimes people hear my daughters' first names and say, "You gave your daughters Celtic names," and I tell those people: "I *wish*." I'd have been happy to call the girls Larry and Chief, but my wife objected, and so instead we gave them Gaelic names: Siobhan and Maeve.

The girls have been typographical terrors literally from Day 1, when the nurse misspelled "Siobhan" on the hospital room whiteboard. As a birth present, the Basketball Hall of Famer Ann Meyers sent Maeve a lovely piece of art that spelled her name . . . *Mauve.* My own father, when Siobhan was born, ordered a silver cup inscribed . . . *Siobahn.*

A grown woman named Siobhan gave me an easy mnemonic for remembering that name: "Tell people it's spelled exactly the way you pronounce it after eight pints of Guinness." And so I do.

For the record, Siobhan is pronounced "shove on," the opposite of "shove off." Maeve rhymes with "rave." I sometimes think it's actually a contraction of "misbehave."

But why *do* this to our daughters, you ask? Why give them names that can be spelled properly only after bouts of binge drinking? The answer has to do with fathers and daughters and sports.

Baseball first. My mother was born Jane Claire Boyle. Her father, Jimmy Boyle, briefly played catcher for John McGraw's New York Giants. He was a second-generation big-league ballplayer—an impressive feat for 1926, at which time there had *been* only two generations of big-league ballplaying.

Jimmy's two uncles, Jack and Eddie Boyle, caught for the Phillies and Pirates, respectively. Jimmy's brother, Buzz Boyle, roamed the Ebbets Field outfield for Casey Stengel's Brooklyn Dodgers.

The Boyle dynasty emigrated from Cork, Ireland, in the 1800s and settled in Cincinnati, the birthplace of my mom *and* of professional baseball—twinned at birth and forever after inseparable.

Throughout my childhood, Grandpa Boyle's framed big-league contract hung in our house next to a photo of him in his Giants flannels. I came home from second grade one afternoon to find Mom dancing on the shag carpet of our family room, and Pete Rose—his sideburns like two shag-carpet samples—circling the bases at Shea Stadium. He'd just given Mom's beloved Reds a 2–1 lead over the Mets in the twelfth inning of Game 4 of the National League playoffs. I had never seen her happier.

Except when she spoke of Ireland, which she never visited, though that was to change in October of 1991, when she and my father were planning to make their first pilgrimage.

In September of that year Mom died, abruptly, of a rare disease called amyloidosis, five weeks before her Ireland trip. My father went anyway, to grieve, and took my only sister, Amy, with him. Fathers and daughters and Cork.

Their trip to the ancestral home of the Boyles meant leaving Minnesota (where my siblings and I were raised) during the Twins' epic seven-game World Series win over the Braves, a Fall Classic that remains a rumor to Dad and Amy, exiled on the Emerald Isle in presumptive honor of my mother's wishes.

But I don't think Mom would have wanted to miss that series in Minnesota—her home of the previous twenty-one years—given her ardor for baseball, passed down from her father, who caught a single inning of a single game on a gorgeous June Sunday at the Polo Grounds in 1926, on that other shimmering island: Manhattan.

~~~

It was on that same island, seventy-five years after my grandfather's glorious half inning, that I met my future wife in an Irish bar on West 79th Street called the Dublin House. Our first date was at a different Irish bar, The Emerald Inn, a few blocks away. These were (and remain) the kind of joints where it's possible to watch soccer broadcast from the British Isles on Saturday mornings while drinking Guinness and eating baked beans off a paper plate.

And so it seemed appropriate, when our first daughter was born on Christmas morning of 2004, to name her Siobhan, an Irish feminine form of John, whose English equivalent is Joan or Jane: my mother's name.

Two years later, when another daughter arrived, we called her Maeve, not at all dissuaded by its literal translation: "intoxicating." Indeed, given the principal sites of our meeting and courtship, my wife and I embraced the etymology of Maeve. Throughout her first year of life, Maeve wore a Onesie from a Chicago bar of the same name, emblazoned with its slogan: MAEVE—SHE WHO INTOXICATES.

For years I imagined watching baseball with my children. And then I had children, who do as they please. I shouldn't have been surprised that the girls, with their pedigrees, liked nothing more from an early age than to curl up next to me on the couch on Saturdays and watch Old World soccer from the other side of the Atlantic— English Premier League games on Fox Soccer Channel and ESPN.

They didn't care for American football, largely because a menacing robot would pop onto the screen at random intervals during Fox's NFL coverage, sending the girls running from the room in terror. What's more, erectile-dysfunction commercials had me leaping on the remote as if it were a live grenade.

Baseball, to the girls, was Hairstyles of the Rich and Famous. They loved the dreadlocks of Manny Ramirez, the facial-hair topiary of David Ortiz. But they couldn't sit still for a Red Sox game, despite the ubiquity of those broadcasts in New England, where we live. Baseball, too, was bedeviled by commercials, and I didn't relish the thought of explaining to them the difference between the leftfielder named Yaz and the birth-control pill of the same name.

So fall weekends became centered around soccer, blessedly free of commercials and homicidal robots. (Unless you count the Manchester United defender Nemanja Vidic. And believe me, we do.)

The English league fit well with the girls' collective preexisting condition: an obsession with London that began with children's books—*Madeline in London* and *Richard Scarry's Busy, Busy World,* and *Mary Poppins* (both the P. L. Travers books and the movie they inspired). Siobhan and Maeve know all about the London Eye and beefeaters and red phone booths. A London Tube map hangs on a wall in our basement, and they can identify the Arsenal stop on the Piccadilly line between Holloway Road and Finsbury Park.

Arsenal is our team. On Siobhan's fourth birthday, Santa brought us all Arsenal jerseys for Christmas. We wear those jerseys, emblazoned FLY EMIRATES, while lined up on the couch, descending in height like bars on a graph. On the wall behind us is a 1932 poster that once hung in the London Underground. I bought it, for more money than I can justify, at a vintage-poster museum in Boston. It reads: HRH THE PRINCE OF WALES WILL ATTEND THE ARSENAL–CHELSEA MATCH NEXT SATURDAY. BOOK TO ARSENAL STATION.

At the time of this writing, Siobhan hasn't turned five and doesn't yet understand all the nuances of the game. She still thinks that Premier League matches end with both teams leaving the stadium on a single red double-decker bus, the winning team on top, the losing team on bottom.

But she knows that Everton plays in Liverpool and that Liverpool is the home of the Beatles. When the first ten notes of a Muzak version of "Strawberry Fields" came on in some office lobby somewhere, Siobhan sang to herself absentmindedly: "Let me take you down, 'cause I'm going to Strawberry Fields." And my knuckle hair stood on end.

And she sometimes picks up on subtleties that I miss, even after twenty years in sports journalism.

"Dad?" Siobhan asked one day in the front yard.

"Yes?"

"Why isn't our grass as beautiful as Arsenal's?"

The Gunners' grass *is* beautiful, and with a little investigation I learned that their head groundsman, Paul Burgess, was a three-time Premier League Groundsman of the Year. Just three months earlier, Burgess had—like every other superstar in world soccer—been hired away by Real Madrid to tend the grass at the Bernabeu. The girls and I agreed it was only right that a man of his horticultural genius should literally seek greener pastures.

Like Burgess, the girls have embraced Spain's La

Liga. They have even dabbled in Italy's Serie A. Maeve woke from a nap one recent afternoon and asked if she could watch *Dora the Explorer*. But when I turned on the TV in preparation to find Nickelodeon, it was already tuned to an AC Milan–Juventus match rerunning on FSC. I was about to change the channel when three-year-old Maeve—like some hopped-up husband on Super Bowl Sunday—snapped, "Leave it!"

I complied, and Maeve, calming down, said softly by way of apology, "I just want to watch soccer." And she sat there, still sleepy-eyed, absorbed in the play of Andrea Pirlo and Filippo Inzaghi and Alessandro Del Piero, names that can't help but make her own feel less exotic.

The girls have always loved to sound out the Arsenal roster, so full of mellifluous handles: Cesc Fabregas, Kolo Toure, Abou Diaby. On their tongues, the name of the Gunners' fabled French manager, Arsene Wenger, becomes one word—Arsonfinger. It sounds like a heavy-metal band or a comic-book supervillain.

"Who's your favorite team?" I asked Siobhan when my wife and I introduced her to Julie Foudy, a former star of the U.S. women's national team. Foudy had just signed autographs for a long line of girls who worshipped the U.S. women's team.

"Arsenal," Siobhan said.

"Arsenal?" said Foudy. "Wow. You picked a good one."

She did. The Gunners are dedicated to stylish, entertaining, beautiful soccer that is sometimes maligned for prizing artistic merit over results. But I love that my daughters esteem these values, implicitly rejecting the inflated payroll of superstar-laden Chelsea.

⁓⁓⁓

Last summer, the girls attended a summer sports camp coached by a college junior from London named Leon. Coach Leon spoke to the baffled three- and four-year-olds in Cockney rhyming slang. "Are you telling porky pies?" he asked one preschooler, who blinked back in incomprehension. I whispered, "That means lies."

The girls loved him. When Coach Leon saw Siobhan in her Arsenal shirt the first day, he said, "Oh, no, Siobhan, not Arsenal! We can't have you on this team! We support Chelsea!"

But Siobhan held fast. "I like Arsenal," she said. There followed a pause, after which she added, "But I also like Chelsea." I reacted with horror, and Siobhan looked to one of her teammates and said, "Because Chelsea is my friend's name."

I realized then that as much as she likes her own name, Siobhan might have preferred to be named for a London soccer team. If we have another girl, I have said, she'll be called Arsenal.

But she won't. I know that now. We've gotten out of the exotic-name business. Siobhan and Maeve recently got a baby brother. His name is Tom, which comes as a kind of relief.

It was something Siobhan said that put the fear of God in me. We were watching Arsenal play Olympiakos in a Champions League match. The announcer had frequent occasion to call the name of the Greek team's

Brazilian midfielder, Dudu. "Doodoo?" Siobhan said the first time she heard it, her eyebrows descending in a V of disapproval. "That's a not-nice name."

Then came the hammer blow: "Why would his dad *do* that to him?"

And I thought: I'm sure he had his reasons.

STEVE RUSHIN *is the author of the novel* The Pint Man *and two nonfiction books,* Road Swing: One Fan's Journey Into the Soul of America's Sports *and* The Caddie Was a Reindeer and Other Tales of Extreme Recreation. *While on staff at* Sports Illustrated, *he was voted National Sportswriter of the Year by his peers. He is a graduate of Marquette, which awarded him an honorary doctor of letters for "his unique gift of documenting the human condition through his writing."*

The first woman to run the Boston Marathon owes it all to a man among men.

OVER THE LONG RUN

~~~

Kathrine (K. V.) Switzer

"Life is for participating, not spectating."
—W. H. SWITZER, 1960

Oh, Gawwwwd, honey. You don't want to be a *cheerleader*! They're so, well, *silly*," my dad said at dinner. Yeah, silly is right; I thought they were pretty brainless too. I mean, they didn't even know the game of football, cheering things like "First and ten, do it again!" when we had just lost the ball. But still, I was going to try out for the junior-varsity cheerleading squad at Madison High School. Being a cheerleader was like having a passport to being pretty, popular, and going out with the captain of the football team. I had frizzy hair, was skinny, wore glasses, and, worst of all, I had no breasts. I was hoping for some kind of miracle transformation, and I thought maybe being a cheerleader would do it.

"I'm not having you hanging around outside locker rooms waiting for boys," Mother said, looking at me over her reading glasses.

"They don't hang around waiting for boys!" I said.

"They do too," said my brother.

Oh, thanks a LOT, I thought. "Do not."

"Do too."

Dad interrupted with "You know, honey, you shouldn't be on the sidelines cheering for other people. People should cheer for *you*. You are a real good little athlete. You love to run and score goals and strategize." Dad was great at flattery when he wanted to convince you to do things his way. I pouted. "The *real* game is on the field. Life is for participating, not spectating. Your school has a girls' field hockey team. You should go out there, play hard, be a leader." It was true I loved to play hard, but the only girls I saw on the teams were such tomboys; nobody would ask them out in a million years. I didn't want to say that, though, as that would make Mother right.

"I don't know how to play field hockey. I would never make the team," I said. This was true too. I'd never had a hockey stick in my hand.

"Well, now, that's easy, kid! All you have to do is get in shape! Just run a mile a day and you'll be in shape by hockey season."

"A *mile*? Run a *mile* a day?!!" Really, I was incredulous. He might as well have told me to go climb Kilimanjaro.

"Look, I'll show you how you can do this." He pulled out a pencil and paper. He began with our yard measurements and showed me how many laps I'd need to do to run a mile.

"I make it seven laps."

I groaned. "That's far."

"You could do it right now, just going out the door. Anyway, you start slowly at first, and over time you'll get better. Heck, I trained a whole battalion and then marched the entire group twenty-five miles a day many a time. And I had to jog up and down the line and carry plenty of laggards' packs for them too, to keep the group together!"

Dad was a handsome six-foot-four colonel in the Army, and when I was a very little girl I used to confuse him with God, because they said God was a big man in the sky looking down on you. But Dad wasn't imperious; he had a warmth and homespun charm that belied his disciplined military success. Really, he was just a grown-up farm kid who went barefoot most of his childhood, rode a horse to school, survived the Great Depression, and managed somehow to wrangle enough jobs to pay his way through college. He—and my mother also—were the first in their families to do so. Of this, he was intensely proud. The gauntlet was always thrown down to both my brother and me: "If *I* did this well, *you* can do even better." It was important that the expectation was for *both* of us; my father made no distinction between my brother and me, and you can bet I was darn proud to be considered an equal.

I could see why my dad was good at motivating the troops. He always managed to show how difficult things could be accomplished bit by bit, and he'd always give some extreme and motivating example that would demonstrate that it was not all that hard anyway. It was a great formula, and the best part was, he would set a challenge for you. "I guarantee you: Run a mile a day all summer long and you'll make that team by autumn." It was also a great diversionary tactic; cheerleading was never brought up again.

I set out the next day to run the seven laps, jogging slowly—shuffling, actually. I felt awkward and breathless and knew I looked stupid. And it was so hot! I was red all over. But I hung on and finished. I did it the first time out, like Dad said I could, and I felt, well, I felt like the king of the hill.

There were several pivotal moments in my life, and that dinner-table conversation with my father was one. He knew that I was lurching awkwardly into high school and, like so many prepubescent kids, struggling with questions of identity, self-esteem, and sexuality. I was facing serious challenges.

One of my biggest had begun when my parents put me in a special accelerated program back when I was five. The problem with starting school when you're so young is that, by the time you get to eighth grade, you're only twelve. While everyone else is reaching puberty, you're still a child. Compounding this, eighth grade was the first year of high school for me—there were no middle schools then—and being in this accelerated program meant that I was taking courses like algebra with seventeen- and eighteen-year-olds. In one class, I sat next to the gorgeous hero-hunk captain of the football team. I don't know who felt more idiotic, he or I, but the point is that many of these kids were young adults preparing for jobs, college, or marriage, and I was still playing with dolls.

Academically, it was the same story. My twelve-year-old mind wasn't ready for some concepts, like the "unknown" of algebra (The unknown what? The great unknown of outer space? The Unknown Soldier?). But what can you do? Being held back a year was not even considered—it was a kind of disgrace in those days, and I couldn't say, "It's too hard," because that just wasn't acceptable at my home, where everyone had come from a long line of pioneers, homesteaders, Depression survivors, and World War II heroes. *Nothing* was allowed to be "too hard." If you had an opportunity, your job was to rise to the challenge and muscle through, which I did, often resorting to rote memorization.

Fortunately, ours was an incredibly supportive family. Every night there were lively conversations at dinner, weekends involved working in the yard together, vacations were long camping trips with tales around the campfire, and, for all our lives, celebrations were happy occasions together. So it was natural that when I started running my mile a day, I got a lot of "Atta girl!"s from them. This was helpful, too, because people—like the milkman or mailman—would see me out running laps around our yard and would knock on the door and ask my mother if I was okay. My girlfriends advised me not to run, because their parents said that I'd get big legs and grow a mustache. We all got used to the fact that my running looked strange to everyone else, but at home I was just fine. Dad never failed to ask how it was going.

The miles built up. Every day. For no explicable reason, one day the mile would be easy and the next it would never end. Most of the time I found myself so lost in thought that I started carrying a piece of chalk so I could mark a tree to keep count of the laps. No matter how hard it was that day or how much I didn't want to run, I always felt better afterward. The best part of every run was at the end, when I had this sharp sense of having accomplished something measurable and definable. I won a little victory every day that no one could take away from me. As the summer drifted on, I looked forward to the coming school term with a new confidence. Not about some remote hockey-team possibility but about myself. I felt really great about me, like I could do anything.

Then it was autumn, school began, and I tried out for the hockey team. Sure, I was nervous; I listened to everything coach Margaret Birch said and followed it to the letter. And an amazing thing happened: Because I didn't get tired, winded, or sore, I learned the skills faster than the other beginners. When we took to the field, I could already run with the best. Wow, how did *that* happen? I made the junior varsity team, there were whoops of joy at home, and I was the proudest girl who ever wore a hockey tunic.

I was also exceedingly grateful. Not quite understanding how physical conditioning worked, I thought I had discovered magic. Fifty years later, I still think it's magic.

I began to believe that as long as I ran, I would keep the magic, but if I stopped, I'd lose it. Which is actually true. I called running my Secret Weapon. I was afraid that if I told others about it, they would think I was nuts about all this magic stuff, so I did it quietly on my own. Having a Secret Weapon gave me the confidence to try other sports. I made the basketball team. Then I found out the Secret Weapon somehow also worked when I wanted to try other activities, like dance committees or the school newspaper.

I began working on the school newspaper because there was so little coverage of the girls' sports teams (some things never change) and I wanted to get us some hype. I loved my team! We all played our hearts out and, despite our different social and economic backgrounds, came to enjoy one another off the field at events beyond the reach of the catty high school cliques.

When I was born, my father filled out the birth certificate and in his excited state misspelled "Katherine," leaving the "e" out of the middle. Friends called me Kathy, which I thought sounded a bit lightweight for a sports byline, while my closest pals called me Switz. I thought that was very cool, but the faculty adviser wouldn't let me use it. "Kathrine" was always changed by the typesetter (yes, they had to set type in those days) into "Katherine," and I got annoyed at seeing my name "corrected" into an incorrect one, so I often used my initials, K. V. Switzer. Initial-signing was in the family anyway—my great-grandfather was W.H., and Dad, also a W.H., signed his name that way. At this time I also was reading—and salivating over—*The Catcher in the*

Rye; J. D. Salinger was a god to me, and fast on his heels came T. S. Eliot and e. e. cummings. It was clear: All strong people and great writers used their initials. I felt very good about becoming "K. V. Switzer, Sportswriter."

By the end of my freshman year, I was tired of being a skinny kid. In one of the millions of magazines my mother stacked up around the house, I found a fascinating article about the caloric values of food and caloric expenditure. The two highest-calorie foods were peanut butter and chocolate, and the article advised eating earlier in the day to expend calories to help weight loss. This made perfect sense to me, so I had a peanut butter and jelly sandwich and a big glass of chocolate milk every night before bedtime. I gained fifteen pounds over the next year and grew nearly four inches. Whether the peanut butter helped puberty or whether womanhood was thundering on anyway, I'll never know, but suddenly I was a woman, and I'll never forget the expression on my father's face when he looked at me one day and then went into the other room to talk to my mother. I overheard only part of their conversation: "Holy cow, when did *that* happen?"

Though I was devoted to keeping fit, I was not passionate about becoming a professional athlete. First, such an opportunity didn't exist for me, and I didn't pine for it the way Billie Jean King did when she was a kid and wanted to play professional baseball. It might have been different, of course, if there had been professional running like there is today. Anyway, I wanted a career that also utilized my education. It's an awful thing to say now, but when I was growing up, there was a feeling that people who earned their living in physical labor—including pro athletes—were to be pitied, because they didn't have either sufficient education or intellect for an executive kind of job. I wanted to keep myself in balance; the Greek concept of strong mind and strong body registered strongly with me.

So did Greek and Roman statuary: I positively ogled the statue of Diana the Huntress; she was athletic *and* feminine *and* self-possessed *and* she had small breasts too, so she was my new role model. I felt as in control of my body as she did, and since guys were beginning to hit on me in school, I was not an easy mark. I didn't need the boys' attention for self-esteem; despite having no sex education, running gave me enough physical confidence to thwart those needy little nerds. There was no doubt; it was thanks to the running, which truly was magic.

By my junior year, I had a boyfriend. Dave was fun; he played center on the football team, and since his dad was the same rank in the Navy as my dad was in the Army, we had a lot in common. Every Friday night after the football game, Dave and his friend Larry the linebacker would come over to our house, tired, happy, and bruised, and we'd make pizza and talk through the game. Often I shared my experiences about a hockey game, and the boys took me seriously. I lived for the annual President's Council on Physical Fitness and Sports day, when, among other events, we were tested on how many sit-ups we could do in a minute (I beat both the guys, with sixty-three) and on the 600-yard run. I was the fastest girl, but I wasn't as fast as the boys, which annoyed me. One evening I pushed Dave and Larry a bit, asking what their acceptable limit for women's exertion was. It was hard for them to define, but finally they agreed that they didn't like it when a woman played so hard she sweated through the back of her shirt. I had no judgmental feeling about this; I was not a heavy sweater myself. Yet.

My educational ambition was to go to a big university, but Dad insisted I go to school in our home state of Virginia and that I attend a coed college, saying that women's schools were effete and unrealistic—something I'm embarrassed to say I agreed with at the time. Incredibly, there were only two coed colleges in the whole state then—William and Mary, which I knew would not accept me with my mediocre SATs, and Lynchburg College, which was smaller than my high school. Dad knew I was disappointed, so as usual he made a deal with me: Since he was paying, the first two years would be his choice, and that was Lynchburg, and then the next two years I could choose if I wanted to transfer. I said yes to Lynchburg, and I could see Dad was confident that, once I was there, I'd love it and not leave.

One of the consolations of going to Lynchburg was that they had a women's field hockey team. It seemed a bit perverse that the big universities didn't have women's sports but the small colleges often did. I thought I should prepare myself for this new team by increasing my running distance. If a mile a day would get me on the high school team, I'd need more to make a college team.

I heard that the boys on the high school cross-country team ran three miles; I'd never heard of anybody running farther than that, so I set three miles a day as my goal. If I could do that, the Secret Weapon would kick into overdrive!

Every evening after my summer job, I would go to my high school track and run laps, adding an extra lap each week to the total. Moving up by increments seemed instinctively right and is a key training principle, as it builds a strong base. It also provided good thinking time, and in one of those "eureka!" moments that occur only while running or in the shower, I saw what I really wanted to do with my career. The thing I loved most next to running was writing for the student newspaper. It had never occurred to me that I could study journalism and combine my two loves. By the end of July, I was running three miles a day. I was coated in sweat, all over, and definitely through the back of my shirt. I felt like king of the hill again.

I did end up loving Lynchburg College, the running and the hockey, but after two years I transferred to Syracuse to concentrate on journalism at the famous New-house School. And, no, there were no intercollegiate sports for women; Big-Time Sports were for men. In a brave moment, I asked the men's cross-country coach if I could run with his squad. I couldn't be official but was welcome to train with them, he said, and the guys were wonderful to me.

Particularly enthusiastic was fifty-year-old Arnie Briggs, the ex-officio team manager. Arnie was the university mailman and a veteran of fifteen Boston Marathons.

He took slowpoke me under his training wing, ran with me, and helped increase my distance. To cajole me through snowy winter runs, he would regale me with great marathon stories. Soon I was in love with the idea of the twenty-six-mile-plus distance and told Arnie I wanted to run Boston too. "A woman can't run the marathon," Arnie answered, explaining that women were too weak to withstand the rigorous distance.

All my father's stories about our pioneering ancestors flew into my head. The women in *my* family had hiked alongside the wagon trains! Weak, my ass! Arnie and I argued, and when I said that a woman named Roberta Gibb had jumped into the Boston Marathon and finished it the year before, he just exploded and said, "No dame ever ran no marathon!"

I realized that Arnie, unlike my dad, believed the old myths about sports making women masculine; he was scared of pushing me too far and didn't want to be blamed for turning me into a monster. But he didn't want to lose me as a training partner either.

"If any woman could do it, I believe you could," he mused. "But you'd have to prove it to me. If you ran the distance in practice, I'd be the first to take you to Boston."

Hot damn, I thought, *I have a coach, a training partner, a plan, and a goal: the biggest race in the world—Boston!!*

Many weeks later, our twenty-six-mile trial run felt too easy for me, and I suggested we run another five-mile loop. After the thirty-one-mile workout, I was ecstatic and threw my arms around Arnie; he passed out cold and woke up saying, "Women have hidden potential in endurance and stamina!" We felt like we'd discovered a new world, and my Secret Weapon now felt like a nuclear warhead.

I signed up for the Boston Marathon as—of course—K. V. Switzer. There was no gender requirement on the application form nor in the rulebook. Arnie, my boyfriend Tom, John from our cross-country team, and I drove to Boston the night before the race. I called Dad before I went to bed; he had no idea what the Boston Marathon was, but even when I told him it was twenty-six miles long, he gave me a cheerful "You can do it, kid, you've done the training!" While Dad did not know the million things that can go wrong in a marathon even under the best of circumstances, he did know that I didn't do things unless I had done my homework. All my life he'd taught me that, and it gave me huge confidence.

The next morning we were all glad for our bulky gray warm-up suits, because the sleet had turned to slushy snow. Everyone looked alike in the bitter gloom, but at the start of the race, all the men around me saw that I was a woman and were wishing me the best. When the starting gun went off, I felt like we were going to Mecca.

Two miles into the race, the press truck passed us and the photographers went nuts, seeing a woman in the race wearing bib numbers. Alongside the truck was a bus carrying the race officials, including the codirector, Jock Semple. Guys on the bus began teasing Jock, saying, "Hey, Jock! There's a girl in your race and she's wearing *numbers*!"

Jock lost his temper and jumped from the bus, ran down the street, and grabbed me, screaming, "Get the hell out of my race and give me those numbers!" He swiped at my front, trying to rip off my pinned-on number. I was so scared that I just tried to run away, but he held me by the shirt. Arnie was shouting, "Leave her alone! I've trained her!" The air was filled with the clicking sound of motor-drive cameras, and the photos were flashed around the world. I was terrified.

Suddenly, Tom, who happened to be a 235-pound former all-American football player, came running full tilt and threw a cross-body block into Jock Semple, which sent him flying through the air. Arnie yelled, "Run like hell!" and down the street we flew.

It was a moment that changed my life and consequently the lives of millions of women—and men—all over the globe. I was determined to finish the race, because I knew that if I didn't, everyone would say women were too weak and were always trying to barge into things they couldn't do. I knew if I quit, it would set women way back, not forward. I *had* to finish, even if I did it on my hands and knees.

One of the great things about running a long distance is that you cannot run and stay mad. Eventually my anger over Jock Semple dissipated, and I began to think about why I was in the race and other women weren't. About why there were no sports scholarships for women or professional teams after college. About why the longest women's race in the Olympics was just 800 meters, a mere two laps of the track. Then the light went on—it was because I'd had an opportunity that other women never had. I had role-model ancestors and a dad who told me I could do anything and showed me how to start running. I had Arnie, who gave me fatherly mentoring and encouragement. I had the cheers from the guys on the team. Other women probably had been discouraged from playing sports all their lives, had been fed the old myths and grew up believing them. It would never occur to them to try to run at all, much less a marathon.

Then I remembered an important thing my dad had told me while I was growing up: "You can't always thank people who help you; the best way to say thank you is to pass it on." For all the distress of the day, running had been wonderful to me, and I felt responsible to help other women feel this good and this powerful too. So somewhere over Heartbreak Hill, about twenty-one miles into the Boston Marathon, I began to see a kind of life mission unfold, and it was to create opportunities for women in running. The only way they could know how powerful they might be was to feel it for themselves.

I finished that Boston, and thirty-four other marathons, eventually winning the New York City Marathon and achieving a world ranking. I began to create opportunities by organizing running events, writing, lobbying, and broadcasting. Eventually, I convinced Avon cosmetics to sponsor my program and we took it global, with an aim to get the women's marathon into the Olympic Games. After a million women in 400 races in twenty-seven countries participated, we were able to convince the International Olympic Committee to include the women's marathon in the 1984 Olympics.

When Joan Benoit ran into the Olympic stadium to

win the first-ever women's Olympic marathon gold medal, I knew it was a turning point in how the world thought about women's capabilities. Not just because 90,000 fans were cheering, but because two billion people around the world saw it on television. *Everyone* knows that 26.2 miles (or 42.2 kilometers) is a long race, and now they knew that if women could do that, they could do anything.

And that has proved correct: There's been an explosion in women's running (there are more women runners now than men runners in the USA!), and the media fame and infusion of prize money has given women runners in many countries economic clout and elevated their social status. Now millions of young girls are growing up with no myths or sense of physical limitations. And women everywhere are experiencing that same sense of empowerment that transforms all aspects of their lives, just as it did for a twelve-year-old girl who thought she'd discovered magic when her dad showed her how to run around their backyard.

In the summer of 2001, as my eighty-six-year-old dad lay dying, I spent hours holding his hand while he talked quietly or just slept. One day, in a kind of confessional tone, he said, "You know how in your speeches you say I told you that life was for participating, not spectating?"

"Yes, of course," I answered. "I've probably said that five hundred times!"

He sighed. "I don't remember telling you that."

Parts of this story are adapted from KATHRINE SWITZER's *2007 memoir,* Marathon Woman. *She is an Emmy Award–winning broadcaster of marathons, the author of* Running and Walking for Women Over 40, *and co-author of* 26.2 Marathon Stories. *She still runs and competes in long events.*

When two relative newcomers to boxing squared off in a women's middleweight bout on June 8, 2001, in Verona, New York, the fight itself was eclipsed by some heavyweight publicity about their dads, Muhammad Ali and Joe Frazier.

THE GROANER IN VERONA

~~~

Bernard Fernandez

No, it wasn't the Thrilla in Manila. No one expected that. But it wasn't the Bona in Verona either—and quite a few people had predicted just that sort of artistic disaster.

Laila Ali's eight-round, majority decision over Jacqui Frazier-Lyde, before a surprisingly loud and involved crowd of 6,500 at the Turning Stone Casino, served mostly to demonstrate that, their inexperience notwithstanding, they are, indeed, their fathers' daughters.

"It was fun," Al Bernstein, the longtime ESPN boxing commentator who conducted the postfight interviews, said of the first pay-per-view card in which women were featured in the main event. "Both women showed grit and determination. They are in the embryonic stages of their boxing careers, sure, but they gave it everything they had and you can't ask for much more than that.

"Are there better women boxers? Yes. Would I just as soon see Christy Martin and Lucia Rijker fight? Yes. But this was fun, it was competitive, and it was hardly a travesty."

Martin, for the past decade the best-known female fighter, is in the area for tomorrow's 12th Annual International Boxing Hall of Fame ceremony in nearby Canastota. At a public workout yesterday, Martin, who has been out of training nearly a month, apologized to spectators for not being at her best, but said, "You'll still see more from me than you will tonight from Laila and Jacqui."

Martin opted to boycott last night's show in protest to the fast-tracking PPV status of the celebrity daughters, but a host of other boxing notables showed up, perhaps because they were curious to see whether Ali (10–0, eight KOs) and Frazier-Lyde (7–1, seven KOs) just had the name or some of the game of their famous fathers, former heavyweight champions Muhammad Ali and Joe Frazier, whose 1970s trilogy is the most celebrated rivalry in boxing history.

They didn't have long to wait. From the opening bell, Ali, twenty-three, and Frazier-Lyde, thirty-nine, flung themselves at each other with intensity, if not a lot of elegance. The first toe-to-toe exchange was initiated seconds into the first round and had fans—the crowd seemed evenly split in its loyalties—on their feet and cheering.

Frazier-Lyde, an attorney and mother of three, seemed to wilt in the middle rounds. Her left eye became puffy in the third round and she seemed almost completely spent by the end of five. But, like Smokin' Joe, she found something in reserve and took the fight to Ali the last two rounds.

Judge Tommy Hicks scored the fight even, 76–76, while Don Ackerman and Frankie Adams favored Ali by 77–75 and 79–73, respectively. The *Daily News* card had Ali ahead, 77–76.

"That a thirty-nine-year-old woman could come back the way Jacqui did is really something," Bernstein said. "Laila is more skilled, but she nailed Jacqui with punches and Jacqui kept coming. Laila kept coming too. They're obviously their fathers' daughters.

"If Jacqui knew how to bend at the waist and throw left hooks, she would have won."

The idea that a Frazier lost because of an unfamiliarity with the left hook is amazing, but not as amazing as the competitiveness of the bout.

"The Ali camp did not want a rematch, but maybe public demand will change that," Frazier-Lyde said. "I feel fantastic. My family is here with me [Joe Frazier was at ringside; Muhammad Ali did not attend because of a previous commitment], and I feel like the winner."

Ali believed she clearly deserved the decision, but she praised Frazier-Lyde for making her fight.

"She's wild," Ali said. "It's always a little surprising when you're actually in the ring with a person fighting that way. I said before the fight there's not going to be a rematch. I also said I was going to knock her out and I didn't do that. I didn't think she was going to get me tangled up like she did."

At the postfight press conference, Johnny McClain, Laila's husband–trainer, said his wife would now "go after some fresh meat." To which Smokin' Joe replied, "What's the matter, is your heart pumping Kool-Aid?"

Clearly, the hearts of the old fighters and their young daughters didn't. They proved that, if nothing else.

BERNARD FERNANDEZ *is a native of New Orleans whose first newspaper job was as a copyboy for the* Times-Picayune *during the summer of 1964. He has been a sportswriter at the Philadelphia* Daily News *for more than twenty years, covering boxing and Penn State football. He served four terms as president of the Boxing Writers Association of America, received the Nat Fleischer Award in April 1999 for lifetime achievement, and was inducted into the Pennsylvania Boxing Hall of Fame in 2005.*

*When you're a dad coaching your daughter's seventh-grade
basketball team, you face far more difficult challenges
than teaching the pick-and-roll.*

THE BALL TOOK A
FUNNY BOUNCE

—⁓⁓⁓—

Rick Reilly

P hil Jackson may have won ten titles coaching in the
NBA. John Wooden may have won ten in college.
Whoop-dee-diddly-doo. If they had to coach the players
I had to coach, they'd have been Burger King managers
within six months.

I'd like to have seen them coach seventh-grade girls.

It's been eight years since I went through it and I still
have the nightmares, the facial tic, the memories.

See, for eleven years all I coached was boys' hoops—
until my daughter entered the seventh grade and they
needed an assistant coach at her school. I agreed happily. And that's when I learned something lasting and

real about seventh-grade girls. They are usually in the bathroom.

In the middle of the first game, I was looking around madly for my best defensive guard to sub in. "Where is she?" I yelled.

"In the bathroom, crying," our little guard in the blue-rectangle glasses said. She was sucking on a Tootsie Pop. "Her friends kicked her out of their group today."

Worse, when one girl ran to the bathroom crying, three girls automatically followed to console her, followed by three others to console *them,* followed by three others who did not really *want* to go in but were merely pulled in by seventh-grade-girl gravitational pull. This would always leave just me and the girl in the blue-rectangle glasses, who would slurp on her Tootsie and shrug.

It was a small school, only twenty girls in the entire class, but they were required to go out for at least one sport, so they came out for basketball. You never had the idea it was more important in their lives than, say, ChapStick.

Still, they came out, bless their hearts. The only slight problem was, most of them had played as much basketball as they had operated forklifts.

For instance, we had a forward who never stopped adjusting her butterfly hair clips, even during our full-court press. And she was our captain. Before the opening tip-off of our first game, she came back from the center-court meeting and announced, "Okay, the ref said whoever wins the tip thingy gets to go toward that basket."

Well, it *would* be an interesting rule.

Another difference between boys and girls: Girls have *many* questions. Our team meetings were sometimes longer than our practices. Apparently girls use team meetings as a chance to process feelings, emotions, and social politics. Whereas boys use team meetings as a chance to give each other wedgies.

We'd have long, emotional deliberations over what would be our huddle cheer and whether or not we should wear matching bracelets. Then one of our best dribblers stood up, took a deep breath, and said, "I have an announcement. I am *NOT* going to bring the ball up this year because last year Sherry got *YELLED* at by everybody because she didn't pass them the ball and I *DON'T* want to get yelled at."

You think Kobe Bryant ever said that to Phil Jackson?

One game, our best rebounder slammed the ball down and stomped off the court. "Everybody's yelling my name and I'm sick of it!" She ran immediately to the bathroom, followed by enough gravitational-girl pull to take off your hat. I turned to my one-stop source for seventh-grade-girl questions—the little guard in the blue rectangular glasses—and made a quizzical face. She popped a Tootsie Pop out of her mouth and said, "She's having her period."

Sigh. You think John Wooden ever had to deal with this stuff?

It was fun. It was rewarding. It was really awkward. When they came off the court, it was very difficult to know how to give them their "good-job" slap. On the . . .

nope. On the . . . nope. I always ended up just tapping them lightly on the top of the head. But not so I messed up their butterfly hair clips.

The girls always had their priorities in order, though: 1) boys; 2) friends; 3) looks; 4) hair fasteners; 5) hoops. I remember we were playing half decent one game—good defense, actual attempts to enter the lane—when suddenly the girls backed off, as though somebody had thrown a demure switch. They were giggling and prancing and whispering stuff to one another while the other team whooshed by them, as by a roadside Applebee's. I looked over at the door to the gym and saw the reason—most of the boys' team had just arrived. We got crushed.

One time, my tallest and shyest girl tried to block an opponent's shot and accidentally hit her on the head. She covered her own mouth in horror with both hands, enabling the girl to drop a layup in without obstacle. I called a time-out and asked what exactly happened. "I thought I hurt her!" she explained.

I believe that started my facial tic.

We lost. We lost a lot. We lost worse than the Falkland Islands. We got creamed our first eight games. One we lost 23–2. Another: 19–1. And yet the girls were over it the second the games ended. Actually, they were usually over it in the third quarter. And win or lose, it did my heart good to see them afterward, heading to the one place they loved to be together and celebrate—the bathroom.

Finally, in our ninth game, all heaven broke loose. For the first time ever, we hit the cutter for a layup. My little shooting guard/five-foot-zero daughter, Rae, hit three running 15-footers. We hadn't even hit three 15-foot *passes* all year, much less a jumper. We came from behind and won in a shoot-out, 16–15, capped by the little guard in the blue rectangle glasses setting the most beautiful screen to free up the winning layup.

In all my years coaching, I never felt more giddy. I threw my clipboard in the air, ran onto the court, and grabbed the shoulders of the little girl in the blue rectangle glasses and screamed, "That was the greatest pick I've ever seen!"

And she yelled, "What's a pick?"

I've run into her and some of the other girls over the years, and none of them went on to play so much as high school basketball. But they remember that seventh-grade season fondly, I guess.

"I loved it," Rae said once. "Especially the matching bracelets."

RICK REILLY *is the back-page columnist for* ESPN The Magazine, *a featured columnist for* ESPN.com, *as well as an essayist for* ESPN SportsCenter, *ESPN golf and tennis coverage, and ABC Sports. He's been voted National Sportswriter of the Year eleven times. He has two sons and one daughter, Rae, who texts approximately 11,000 times as fast as he does.*

*Whom can a baseball promoter turn to when his daughter
is facing blindness? In Mike Veeck's case, his late father,
legendary sportsman Bill Veeck, who never let a little
disability get him down.*

SIGHT UNSEEN

~~~

Mike Veeck with Pete Williams

We avoided the decision for years, but now my wife,
Libby, and I were leaving our seventeen-year-old
daughter, Rebecca, off at the Florida School for the Deaf
and the Blind.

We drove slowly into the seventy-two-acre campus
along the Intracoastal Waterway in St. Augustine, Florida.
The 113-year-old school with 750 students was where
Ray Charles had once learned to read Braille. We sighed
at the unencumbered water view—a perspective Rebecca, like many of the students, would never enjoy.

It was February 9, 2009, more than a decade since
Rebecca had been diagnosed with a form of retinitis pig-

mentosa called cone-rod dystrophy, which causes blindness. For a while, she could turn her head ninety degrees and catch you out of the corner of her eye. Over time, even that disappeared.

Aside from the gradual deterioration of her eyesight, Rebecca has led a normal childhood—horseback riding, dancing, reading, learning karate, playing music, swimming, surfing, and traveling. Like three previous generations of Veecks, she has worked in baseball, helping wherever needed for the Charleston RiverDogs, one of the six minor-league teams my partners and I own.

She even remained in a regular public school, working twice as hard with tutors and computer devices to help her complete her work. That was the easy part. The bigger challenges were the kids who would sneak up from behind and push her or wet down bathroom floors so she would fall.

Rebecca insisted on staying mainstreamed, not wanting to be different. We should have made her change schools when we started to have a tutor four days a week to keep up with the workload. Later, as her peers began driving and becoming more independent, Rebecca felt more isolated.

Still, Libby and I resisted schools for the blind, never broaching the topic with Rebecca. One school we visited seemed so dark and institutional, Libby left in tears. But by the midpoint of her junior year of high school, Rebecca was ready. The teachers seemed too busy, her fellow students less accommodating.

"I'm done putting my foot forward and trying to get people to understand," Rebecca told us. "I'll go anywhere. Just get it done."

We found a gem at the Florida School for the Deaf and the Blind, where many faculty members have served for decades. The forty-seven buildings remind me of a small, tight-knit university—perhaps the sort of school Rebecca soon will attend.

As we drove away from the school, emotions swirled. We were doing the right thing, we were sure of that. Should we have enrolled her earlier? Would that have helped? Could we have approached the last ten years differently?

Out of nowhere, I remembered it was February 9, my dad's birthday. Bill Veeck had been dead for more than two decades, and even so he had been providing a blueprint for how to respond to her situation all along.

When Rebecca was first diagnosed, I struggled with how to deal with her. Thankfully, I had my old man to draw upon for inspiration.

Rebecca knew all the stories about Dad's tenure as a baseball owner. She knew about the exploding scoreboard at old Comiskey Park, and how he once sent the midget Eddie Gaedel to bat for the St. Louis Browns, and how Dad grew ivy on the walls at Wrigley Field. She also knew Dad had lost a leg in World War II and that he didn't let that slow him down.

I challenge you to find a sad Bill Veeck story. Not a poignant one or a moving one, but a truly sad one. They don't exist. And that's why I've used Dad as my model for this.

I told Rebecca about how Dad poked fun at himself. About how he would gather all the neighborhood kids around, drive a nail through his wooden knee, and tell them to go home and ask their fathers to do the same.

About how each spring he would paint his wooden leg bronze and then spend the rest of the summer trying to tan his body to match. About how his kids, especially me, would hide his wooden leg from him.

So with his help, Rebecca and I learned to laugh about her dreadful disease. Not long after she was diagnosed, she and I developed the R.P. song.

"Retinitis," she would sing.

"Pigmentosa," I would croon back.

In those early days, Rebecca bumped into things on purpose just to get a few laughs, though of course she also bumped into them unintentionally. Rebecca and I went on rides on a tandem bicycle and I'd tell her to take the lead. At the ballpark, Rebecca starred in between-inning skits, sat in the dunk tank and egged on fans, worked the phones, and served as an all-around ambassador of fun, putting everyone at ease.

I'm not going to say there's a silver lining to any of this, though we're happy that the Veeck name and Rebecca's willingness to talk to the media have drawn attention to the disease, raised money for research, and hopefully helped expedite the search for a cure.

When Rebecca was diagnosed, Libby and I figured we would have to show her how to deal with the disease. In fact, over the last decade, it's been quite the opposite. She's shown us, and others, how to handle it.

A few years after the diagnosis, we were having a family dinner out with friends. Rebecca asked to be excused and walked over to a nearby table, where a man was sitting by himself.

She was far enough away that we couldn't hear the

conversation. Given her outgoing personality, I assumed she must have known the man.

"Who was that, Rebecca?" I asked when she returned fifteen minutes later.

"Just someone who looked a little lonely," she said. "I thought he needed someone to talk to."

I looked over to the table and the man was wiping away a tear, as was one of our dinner companions.

Libby and I have learned so much from Rebecca. As a whole we're a nation of whiners, but Rebecca rarely complains about her predicament. I can't think of anything scarier than going without eyesight. I'll close my eyes as I walk through an airport or hotel and wonder how she does it.

I used to beat myself up for Disco Demolition Night, the infamous promotion I staged in 1979 for the Chicago White Sox that caused a near-riot at Comiskey Park and derailed my career in Major League Baseball. Even though I later had success as a minor-league operator, I waited nearly twenty years for a second chance in the majors. And when I did get that opportunity, I resigned after only seven months. As much as I treasured the opportunity to work for the Tampa Bay Devil Rays, it didn't seem that important compared to being with Rebecca.

I've never believed in reincarnation, but I've been giving it some careful consideration because of Rebecca. Like Dad, she's blue-eyed and blond, fair-skinned, and left-handed. If you look at her from the nose up, the resemblance is eerie. She has endless curiosity and varied interests. I can see her performing on Broadway, working for a nonprofit, or even becoming a fourth-generation baseball operator.

Like Dad, she puts people who might not know how to handle her ailment at ease. She understands that she is a nonsighted person in a world of sight, but she's not averse to throwing out self-deprecating lines.

"Not a bad throw for a blind girl," she'll say.

It's not meant to solicit sympathy or even a response. It's just her way of dealing with it. You'd think there would be more anger or resentment, but somehow she manages to channel it into something else.

"Deep down, my grandfather and I are very much alike," Rebecca says. "I feel like there's a part of him in me. He never let having one leg slow him down or keep him from having fun. That's why, while I accept that I'm blind, I never totally accept it."

Rebecca and I don't joke as much about her condition these days. The R.P. song was shelved, and I take my cues more from her when it comes to poking fun at the situation. I suppose it's partly the normal evolution of the father–daughter relationship that comes with the teenage years, but it's also the reality of the situation as Rebecca's vision has deteriorated. We are still hopeful for medical advances that might allow Rebecca to see— some recent advances are promising for the long term.

These days, I run minor-league clubs and am fortunate to travel the country speaking to various groups. Rebecca's strength and ability to laugh even in the face of adversity have made me realize that Fun Is Good is much more than just the marketing philosophy behind how we run the ball clubs. It's a message that provides much of the fodder for my talks—especially in these difficult economic times. We *all* need to laugh more.

Rebecca is thriving at the Florida School for the Deaf and the Blind, though we miss her terribly during the week. Soon she'll be off to college, where she'll no doubt thrive in whatever course of study she pursues.

That's because, though she may be lacking in eyesight, her vision for the future is clear.

MIKE VEECK *is president and part owner of six successful minor-league baseball teams. Son of the late Hall of Fame club owner Bill Veeck, he has followed his father's lead, with innovative promotions that have captured national attention. He coauthored* Fun Is Good: How to Create Joy and Passion in Your Workplace and Career *with Pete Williams. He lives in Mt. Pleasant, South Carolina.*

They're twins, and they're athletes, but they're not exactly the same. Vive la différence!

GRRRRRRR

～⌇～

Steve Wulf

Among the hundreds of baseball caps in our house—yes, dear, I'll get rid of them soon, I promise—are a pair of Elizabethton Twins hats. We've never been to Elizabethton, Tennessee, to watch Minnesota's Rookie League affiliate, but it just so happens that the cap has an "E" superimposed over a Twins logo. And we happen to have twin girls whose first names begin with an "E."

They are both smart, athletic, beautiful, courteous, slightly spoiled, and deeply loved by their grandparents, parents, older brothers, and each other—though they would never actually admit that last devotion.

They are fraternal twins, which means they are not identical. And how. You would not know they were even sisters to look at them. For one thing, their facial features are separated by the Baltic Sea: Elizabeth gets hers from Mom's Scandinavian family on the west side, Eve from Dad's ancestors on the east side. For another, Eve is the taller; Elizabeth, the lower center of gravity. Eve is right-handed, Elizabeth, left-handed. To think that we once dressed them in the same clothes now seems slightly comical. A few years ago, for a sixth-grade history project, Elizabeth constructed a replica of the Fenway Park Green Monster; Eve chose to celebrate Christian Dior's first collection in 1947. Also, Elizabeth uses Clairol Herbal Essences Hello Hydration shampoo, and Eve likes Clairol Herbal Essences Drama Clean.

In matters of sports, they have chosen decidedly different paths. Eve has or had field hockey, softball, and horseback riding all to herself. Elizabeth has claimed ice hockey, lacrosse, and baseball as her own. They both did basketball; they both do soccer. Little wonder we have two cars with 300,000 miles between them and the washer/dryer repair guy on speed dial.

Now, within every parent there is a certain reluctance to compare siblings. After all, we love them each infinitely (this much!), and we strive to give each equal amounts of quality time. But it became apparent fairly early that one of the girls was a better athlete than the other.

Come to think of it, we saw it at birth. Throughout my wife's pregnancy, Eve was Baby A because she was in front of the womb, and Elizabeth was Baby B. But when my wife went into premature labor seven weeks early and a few days into a vacation, Elizabeth somehow elbowed her way to the front to claim seniority by two minutes. Even then, she could forecheck.

Before I go on, I need to make one thing clear here. Eve is a good athlete, a very good athlete actually. It's just that Elizabeth is gifted. She basically kicked the butts of the boys in nursery school. In kindergarten, she so excelled at after-school floor hockey that the gym teacher, who also doubled as the local high school's varsity ice-hockey coach, told my wife we had to put her on skates. Like right away.

The girls played soccer together in Kinder Kickers. After one Saturday session, we were sitting in the local coffee shop for lunch when a woman came up to the table and said, pointing to Elizabeth, "I saw you at soccer. You are amazing. You are going to the Olympics." My eyes immediately went to Eve, who was sitting across the table from her twin, in an identical soccer uniform. I was hoping she wasn't paying attention. Ah, but she was. Out of this angelic little blond girl I heard what can only be transcribed as *"Grrrrrrr."*

Her growl was not directed at her sister, nor even at the clueless lady, but rather at the unfairness of it all. Even at the tender age of five, she knew she was being overshadowed.

Fortunately, the girls had already begun to choose separate sports: For their seventh birthday, Eve got a riding helmet, Elizabeth, a hockey helmet. But they still had soccer in common. I loved those days. I coached them both, and every once in a while I would stop the car at a park, roll out the soccer ball, and watch them kick and pass to each other. It's very hard to get second- and third-graders to pass the ball, but in our local rec league, we won the coveted Pelé Cup largely because Eve and Elizabeth were always looking for each other.

But then, like the serpent in Eden, travel soccer came along. In our community, tryouts are considered a sacred rite, and the coaches who do the evaluations think of themselves as high priests. After a couple of hours of silly drills, they hand down their pronouncements: A Team, B Team, Sorry. When we got the call, we were told Elizabeth had made the A Team, Eve, the B Team. (Ah, A and B again.)

Subsequent years would expose many of those original assessments as faulty—one of the best players in town was a Sorry. But we were told the decisions of the judges were final. Had I been wiser, I would have insisted that the girls play together on the B team. Instead, I followed along like a sheep.

(A word of advice to parents of multiples: Listen to your kids, not some coach who may be separating them just because he/she can. If the kids want to stay together, tell the coach. Chances are that he/she will choose a package deal over a squad without the player already penciled in at center mid.)

So our next few autumns and springs were spent with two different soccer teams, schedules (games and practices), and coaches. That wasn't the hard part. What was particularly difficult was the realization that the on-field chemistry between twin sisters had been lost. At one point Eve worked her way up to a spot on the

A Team, but she was miserable standing on the sidelines and chose to go back to her old team. I didn't blame her in the least.

If there is an imbalance in talent between the two girls, there is none in determination. *Grrrrrrr* is a gift unto itself, and they both have it. Elizabeth's pitching brought me, her coach, my only championship in twenty-one seasons of coaching Little League. She was the only girl and only third-grader on a Squirt hockey team that played in the state tournament. But my favorite sports memory of her is from a heartbreaking loss: She sees a runner break from third as she walks back to the mound with the ball, runs toward the third-base line, and dives to tag him out before he can score the winning run.

One of Eve's finest moments also came in defeat. She was pitching in a softball championship game when the defense collapsed behind her. It wasn't just the fielders who betrayed her. One of her best friends walked over to the other side of the field to avoid Eve and hang out with the team that was winning. When it came time for Eve to bat, she wiped away her tears, consolidated her sobs into a deep breath, and walked to the plate. First pitch, fastball. She smoked a triple down the left-field line.

That was a few years ago. The other day, both girls had soccer games a half hour apart, a quarter mile apart. Dropped Elizabeth off for warm-ups. Took Eve to her pregame. Drove back to watch Elizabeth's first half—she scored! Turned around for Eve's game—she scored! Ducked out at the half to watch Elizabeth's team finish off its victory. Hurried her off the field so we could watch the end of Eve's game.

When we got there, the score was tied 1–1. With just a few minutes remaining, Eve dribbled the ball down the left side, fairly deep, then passed it to a knot of team-mates in front of the net. One of them knocked it in for a 2–1 win over a team that had beaten them 5–0 earlier in the season. Quite naturally, all the glory centered around the goal-scorer: the mob of teammates, the calls of glee, the tribute dancing, the parental compliments after the game.

Nobody went over to Eve. As I met her coming off the field, I could sense the *grrrrrrr* rising from within.

Just then Elizabeth came over. "Nice cross, Eve!" she said, and Eve smiled.

Together once more.

STEVE WULF *is the editor-in-chief of ESPN Books. He is the father of four pitchers.*

Hanky alert: In this 1992 encounter, a reporter shares a paternal bond of baseball and bereavement with a Minnesota Twin.

HEROES

~~~

Ann Bauleke

Partway through the last home stand [in mid-August], when the doctor said my father would probably not live another week with the cancer, the Twins' struggle to stay in the pennant race seemed unimportant. Kent Hrbek and I had planned to talk about his and the Twins' slump, but I missed the interview. For the first time in the month my father had been sick, he had asked me not to leave his side. So I stayed with him until he drifted into a deep, morphine-induced sleep and then raced sixty miles from the hospital in Le Sueur and arrived late at the ballpark. As it turned out, Hrbek had missed the interview too. The shoulder he'd injured the night before had needed treatment.

It's ten years this September since Hrbek's dad, Ed, died at age fifty-three of ALS, the central nervous system affliction known as Lou Gehrig's Disease. Hearing my father's prognosis, a writer friend suggested I talk with Hrbek and write about Hrbek and his dad, and my dad and me. After all, it was our dads who gave us baseball. Hrbek was willing, but we'd had no chance to talk, until I finally reached him by phone in Detroit last week.

Eleven years ago, Kent Hrbek was a first baseman on the Twins' A-ball team in Visalia, California, when his dad phoned to tell him he had ALS. "I didn't know what the hell it was," Hrbek says. "He told me it would kill him, but he didn't know when." Hrbek wanted to quit baseball and go home, but his father told him to stay put. "You've wanted to play baseball your whole life," he said. "We'll come out to visit you."

At the end of August 1981, Hrbek was called up from Class A to the big leagues. "I was supposed to be happy and excited, and my dad was dying," he says. "What are you supposed to do? How are you supposed to act? I told a lot of people I went from the highest to the lowest."

The next year, his rookie season as the Twins' first baseman, the dissonance between his love for his father and his love for baseball continued. "It was weird because I was living out a dream, playing baseball," he explains. "I was getting a paycheck that jumped from $500 a month to $30,000 for a summer. That was like cloud nine. I was Kent Hrbek. I was king of the world, playing in my hometown, experiencing all kinds of things in one year. It wasn't easy."

His father tried to make it easier. "The middle of the summer, we were sitting on the bed in his bedroom," Hrbek recalls. "He told me, 'I'm proud of you and of what you're doing. Don't worry about me. Just keep on playing baseball and having fun. And take care of Mom.' "

———

Hrbek's father encouraged him to go on with life. That's only right as a parent of a twenty-one-year-old. At age forty-two, I didn't think I should need those words from my father. I'd never waited for them before. I'd always forged ahead, sometimes against his silent wishes. Reluctantly, my dad had bid me goodbye on many adventures. I'd gone to Europe twice, once for school and once on a bicycle trip; I'd hitchhiked to California to camp three weeks in the Sierras; I'd spent five months in the desert in Arizona; and I'd lived a year in New Zealand.

These separations seemed necessary. I had grown up feeling responsible for my father's happiness. I never stopped wanting to make him happy and believed falsely that it was a commentary on me when he wasn't. I realized later that the pressure and guilt I'd put on myself only added to the distance between us. After I started writing about baseball, I sent him my articles but asked him not to show them to anyone. Last week, after he died, I found out he'd ignored my request. I'm told he rode his red moped around the neighborhood—this, at the age of eighty—and shared my stories with his friends. I'm glad now that he didn't listen to me and sorry that I tried to censor any joy he took in my work.

The point is, I was used to living a self-centered life. When I learned that he was dying, it was hard to know how to stop. But I followed my impulse, my conflicted urge to be with him. So my father and baseball comprised the past month of my life.

He was a great Twins fan. When he stopped listening to the games and reading the sports pages, I knew he was terribly ill. But baseball still connected us. I gave him the 1991 World Series pin the Twins recently distributed, and he wore it on his pajama collar. Lately, I had to tell him almost every day that the Twins had lost again, while the A's had won. He'd draw his mouth in a line and, without a word, slowly shake his head. When the Twins fell seven games out of first place, he simply said, "They're done."

———

By August of 1982, Ed Hrbek could no longer walk up the steps in the Metrodome, but he continued to attend every home game. I remember seeing him carried down to his seat behind home plate. It was late in the season when the Twins were in Kansas City that Kent Hrbek received the call to come home. That evening, he visited his dad in the hospital. "He was staring into space," Hrbek remembers, "but he knew I was there. He asked me how my knee was. It'd been bothering me, I guess. The next morning, two minutes after I got there, he was gone."

In Hrbek's locker at the Metrodome, there's a photograph of Ed. He's laughing with a friend at someone's retirement party. "It fits him perfectly," Hrbek says. "He always had a smile on his face, unless he was chewing me out for something." The photo also captures Hrbek's one regret. "I never really got to know him as I wanted to," he admits. "I think you really get to know someone when you can sit someplace and talk. He was my baseball coach, and I knew him as my dad, but I never really was an adult hanging around with him. I never had a rip-snorting time with my dad. I know I would have liked to, because I've done it now with his brothers. We've had some serious laughs. They say, 'I wish Ed would've been here.' That's the thing I really miss."

The times Hrbek feels the loss are many: He feels it when teammates bring their dads into the clubhouse; he feels it when off-season hunting and fishing invitations come in; and he feels it when he drives by the shore of Lake Minnetonka, where he and his dad used to fish for crappies.

When I think of my dad, I see him at Johnny's Red & White, the grocery store he owned for most of his working life. He was a svelte six-foot-one. He wore a long white apron and kept a number-two pencil behind his ear. During the 1960s, we attended dozens of Twins games, courtesy of the store's bubblegum vendor. My dad had told him of me, his daughter, a baseball fanatic.

So, like Hrbek, my love of baseball came through my father. Baseball and oil changes were the extent of our conversations. Fifteen years ago he had a cancerous larynx removed, which made conversation even more difficult. But the truth is, neither of us was much of a talker anyway. We "talked" mostly in letters, writing once a week, ever since I left for college. If I missed a week, he'd shake a veritable fist at me in his next note.

The other night when I returned from the hospital, I searched frantically for any letters I might have saved. There they were, in a file with photos and other keepsakes. His letters were distinctive for his squarish printing, which always made me believe he was an artist at heart. "Kinda glad baseball season is here," he wrote in one letter. "Something to listen to." Another time: "I really enjoyed Hrbek's comments on Viola's agent. Hrbie says he'll be here next year and won't be fighting for a couple of bucks. Hooray for Hrbie." He ended one letter telling me, "Well, be calm."

Last week, on August 31, after speaking with Hrbek on the phone, I went to be with my dad. His eyes were shut. His breathing was more labored than it had been the day before. I pulled a chair up next to his bed and took his hand. I told him I was there, that I'd just interviewed Kent Hrbek and would be writing about him and his father, and me and mine.

Hospital staff came in at various times. We'd become acquainted during the short time my dad was sick. That afternoon, sitting by his bed, I talked with one of the hospice women about my relationship with my dad and the one I'd always thought I wanted—one more verbal, a father divulging wisdom to ease a girl through life. I said that now I realize he gave me more than words. He'd given himself: a gentle, simple, quiet man. There were bad times, I admitted. There was alcoholism. But he hadn't had a drink in twenty years. During the past month, what barriers remained had come down a little.

He'd asked me to comb his hair because the comb felt good on his scalp. He'd asked me to pound his back to help him breathe. In these ways, these last days at least, we could be close.

When I was alone with him again, his eyes opened slightly. I stood up, thinking he was awake. All of his energy seemed concentrated on taking one breath. I remembered when I was tiny, resting on his chest, riding up and down with his breathing while he napped in his chair.

"It's hard to breathe, isn't it?" I said now, stroking his arms and shoulders. "It must be scary." Suddenly, I knew he was fading. My hands trembled as I continued to touch him. "It's all right," I told him over and over.

I felt almost panicked, but I stayed with him, holding his hand. I couldn't believe he was giving me this. I couldn't believe he was letting me help him die. "Be peaceful, Dad," I said. "You can let go."

His chest stopped laboring, and his breathing grew shallow. I told him I loved him, and I heard myself asking him to watch over me. A nurse stepped into the room. "I think he died," I whispered. He took two more quick breaths. The nurse checked his heart, and nodded. I sat there a while longer, not wanting to let go of his warm hand.

ANN BAULEKE's *work has appeared in regional magazines and small press weeklies. She is currently working on a collection of personal essays titled* The Man in My Life: A Girl's Affair With Major League Baseball. *She lives in Minneapolis.*

Absent fathers, precocious six-year-olds, miracle outs:
One man discovers the joys, and lessons, of T-ball.

PRACTICE SWINGS

Eric Neel

Hey, Dad.

Your granddaughter and I play T-ball these days at a local rec center, a patch of trampled grass and dirt just north of where the 134 cuts from Pasadena to L.A.'s west side. Tess wears number 12 and meticulously pulls the front of her red jersey down over the top of her pants so you can read ANGELS across the front. She has rituals. She runs out to play second base and draws a broad circle in the dirt with her right toe and then steps into the circle, crouches down, reaches her glove toward the ground, and looks up at the hitter. In the batter's box, she licks her upper lip, taps the plate twice, takes two deliberate practice swings, then pulls the bat up and back until her chin and nose are tucked behind her left shoulder, like she's got a secret, like she's The Shadow peering from behind his cape.

I help coach the team, and she and I practice hitting in the backyard at home sometimes. At the start, I'll wrap my arms around her from behind and put my hands on hers so we can swing the bat together. We're close enough to hear each other breathe, and I'll whisper to her: "Watch the ball all the way. Swing through." When I was her age, you and Mom had already split up; you'd moved out, and the divorce was pending. I remember taking practice swings in front of a mirror in my bedroom, trying to hold the bat still at the finish, trying to imagine what I should look like. So much can go wrong at the beginning. Your arms aren't quite strong enough to bring the bat level through the zone. Your feet get anxious. You lose your balance. So I like to wrap my arms around Tess those first few swings and move through them with her. I like to whisper in her ear.

She's become a pretty good hitter. Lets it fly on contact, even rolls her wrists a little bit. The other day before a game, she told me she knows now how it feels when you hit it right. When I asked her to explain, she put a ball on the tee, drilled it out past second base, then turned to me and said, "That's the way it should feel, right, Daddy?" I was looking for words, something we could talk through and reinforce, but she was flexing other muscles. I wanted to understand what she had learned and how she had learned it. Which bit of my advice had been sage? Which suggestion had been heard? But she just wanted to hit.

Later that same day, when she was experimenting with a new pigeon-toed stance in the third inning of our game against the Blue Jays, I reached down to square her foot to home plate and she stepped back. She brought the barrel of the bat to the ground, put both hands on the knob, like Chaplin's Tramp with his cane, looked up at me with a sweet patronizing smile I thought I would be spared until the teenage years, and said, "Daddy, you just don't understand how I want to live my life." Cracked me up. But caught me short too. She's only six. It's easy to see the green in her. Maybe sometimes I'm missing what she already knows. I think it's easy to see myself—when I was still green—in her too. Maybe sometimes I'm telling her what to do because I wished you could have told me more. Maybe I'm coming to T-ball looking for some sort of salvation. Maybe I should remember to let pigeon-toes pigeon.

On Monday night, our centerfielder lost his hat chasing a ball through the outfield grass. He picked up the ball, and I shouted, "Throw home! Throw home!" but he ran with it. Not toward home plate but in a wicked serpentine motion, chasing after the hat. He finally picked it up as the runner was rounding third, and I shouted again, "Throw home! Throw home!" He stopped, dropped his glove and the ball, put on the hat, pulled it snug, and then picked up the ball and ran it the rest of the way to home plate, where he did not, alas, find the runner. When the next batter came up, Tess held her glove to her face as if it were a hockey mask. From my position behind her on the right-field grass, I shouted, "Take your glove down, T!" "I can't," she replied. "Why not?" I asked. "My lips itch," she explained. Of course they do. "Can you play through it?" I asked. "I think so," she said. "With my glove up." Check and mate.

You teach the kids where first base is. You teach them to hit and to throw and, when the gods smile upon you, to catch. You want to pass on tools, to gird them for what's to come. But you don't coach T-ball so much as you experience it, surrender to it. It has a way of forcing its kids-do-the-darnedest-things Zen on you, of knocking you off your moorings, one unpredictably behatted head and itching lip at a time.

The first time I can remember playing catch with you, you had come to visit at an apartment where I lived with Mom. It was that low-slung, pale cinder-block building with a strip of yellowed grass out front. I fixed you a plate of powdered-sugar mini donuts and a coffee mug full of milk. Remember that? Then we went outside and tossed the ball around. I don't think I caught anything. When you had to go, I stood on the curb watching you drive off, wishing we could play again the next day. Thirty-five years later, I felt the tug of that afternoon while playing catch for the first time with Tess on the T-ball field. Her wayward throws and squinting efforts to catch seemed to echo mine. But that was the game locked up in memory, that was me holding on to a little boy's sadness, rubbing some old jagged keepsake in my pocket.

Tess prefers to play catch with a sock ball thrown

back and forth across the living room. She can snag it out of the air, and she likes to throw it high over my head and see how far I can reach. We're just goofing, trying not to knock over a vase, but we're connecting too. And letting go. "You know, Daddy," she said the other day, "this is our best game."

Outs in T-ball are little miracles. The ball comes fast when you're small. You have to learn to read its path and meet it not where it is but where it'll be. You have to trust you can handle the hurt if you take one on the chin. We've been working on staying low to the ground and moving her feet. I'm teaching the shuttle step—feet apart, then together, then apart—but Tess favors a scissors kick, crossing one leg over the other. She falls about half the time, ends up reaching for the ball from her knees as if she's crawling through the desert looking for water. I think she secretly likes getting dirt on her uniform, likes standing up and brushing herself off.

But you should have seen her in our last game, Saturday morning against the A's. She put it all together just the way we'd been talking about. In the second inning, she was playing second base with a runner on first and two outs. The kid up to bat was a monster—belly like Fat Albert, swing like Pops Stargell—and he hit a screamer to her right. It was going through to the outfield. It was going to roll for days. Only it didn't. She floated to the ball and got her glove down. Timed it perfectly. Scooped it on one hop, brought the glove to her chest, and kept running to step on second base and end the inning. Her teammates ran to the dugout celebrating, but she stayed out there, standing on the bag, clutching the glove and ball. I watched her from near the backstop. Beaming. Feeling the sun. Breathing in the sweet dusty tang of her triumph.

God, I wanted to hold on to that moment. She was a ballplayer in that moment. I was a coach. We had it nailed. But there was more game to play. The next time the monster came to bat, Tess was in the middle of the diamond, in the pitcher's spot, and she took a ball hard off her right forearm. She came off the field crying at the end of the inning.

I told her it was great the way she put her body in front of the ball. She told me she never would have stood there if she thought there was any chance she'd get hit and looked at me like I should have warned her.

I knelt down and hugged her. Wiped her tears.

I told her she was brave—because I believed it and because I wanted her to believe it too. But it was everything I could do not to pick her up and take her home, not to tell her we could play again the next day.

She shook it off. She loves to hit, even with tear-stained cheeks and a purple welt on her arm. I waited for her in the box, put my arms around her and my hands on her hands, ready for our practice swing. She wriggled her shoulders and hips a bit and inched her feet closer to the tee, just out of my grasp.

"I got it, Daddy," she said. "I like the part when you hold my hands." She paused, turned her head over her right shoulder, and added, "But only until I don't need you."

"Okay, Tess," I whispered, and backed up. Watched her swing through.

Made me wonder, who's coaching whom?
See you soon . . . Love, E

ERIC NEEL *is a senior writer for ESPN.com and* ESPN
The Magazine. *He lives in Sierra Madre, California,
where Tess is now learning to be a softball pitcher.*

It's been said that parenting is a marathon. In this case,
it's actually a triathlon.

MY FATHER, THE CHEATER

—⋙⋘—

Kathryn Bertine

I cheated," my father says, panting slightly. We are at
the finish line of the 2005 Escape From Alcatraz
triathlon, which my sixty-eight-year-old dad, Peter
Bertine, has crossed after almost four hours of athletic
effort. After swimming 1.5 miles from the famous
prison island of Alcatraz to the shore of San Francisco's
Crissy Field, then cycling eighteen miles of the notori-
ously hilly city, and topping it off with an eight-mile run
over streets, trails, and sand, I attribute my dad's cheating comment to temporary postrace disorientation.
With perhaps just a smidgen of dementia. My father,
cheat? This is a man who turns his head *and* shields his

eyes if an opponent drops one of their Scrabble tiles on the floor. Not to mention, it is pretty difficult to cheat in a triathlon.

"How?" I laugh. "Did someone give you a ride?"

"Yes," he says.

February 1986. 4:45 a.m. My father's car has a thermometer that bleeps out a crisp ding! *when the outside temperature falls below thirty-four degrees. My father starts the car. The* ding! *is immediate. It is a bitter New York winter morning. I am eleven, and my dad is driving me to figure-skating practice. For six years, until I can drive myself, he will take me to my beloved, freezing, half-outdoor Murray's Rink every day at five o'clock in the morning. He will pick me up two hours later, with a chocolate chip muffin and an iced tea from the vending machine in the rink lobby. He will watch me skate, giving me the thumbs-up through the Plexiglas after each maneuver I attempt. I point upward through the Plexiglas, reminding him not to stand under the rafter with the pigeon's nest. This is our routine.*

The waters of San Francisco Bay are known for three things: frigidity, rough currents, and great white sharks. A delightful trilogy of complications for the bizarre tastes of an endurance athlete. On the remarkably beautiful, clear, warm June day of my father's race, sharks and water temperature are not factors. The current is another story. As is often the case with open-water events, swimmers pick out a target on shore to "sight," or help keep them in line while they swim. Sometimes it is easier to follow the swimmer who's leading, provided they are sighting correctly. When the seven competitors of my father's age group (sixty-five- to sixty-nine-year-old men) jumped into the water among the 1,500 younger triathletes, the collective of wetsuit-clad seniors smartly swam their own pace. It wasn't until the rescue boat pulled up alongside them that my father realized no one had been sighting properly, and their whole tribe had drifted so far off course that the Golden Gate Bridge was almost within grasp. The boat picked up the seven sexagenarians, brought them back to the exact spot where they'd drifted off course, and kindly redeposited them into the water rather than disqualifying the entire age group. While the rules of triathlon have a strict "no outside assistance" policy, the race directors find no fault with this particular situation. My father, however, still believes he cheated by accepting the rescue-boat ride. I console him by offering an alternative perspective.

"I don't think it's cheating if you race *more* than anyone else, Dad," I say, as we check the results. "Besides, if the finish line were in Japan, your age group would have won." He finished toward the back of the sixty-five- to sixty-nine-year-olds, which is just fine with him. He gives me a sweaty hug and asks, "How was your race?"

September 1994. Freshman year of college. I am recruited to run for Colgate University. I have an argument with the coach. In the first month, she dismisses me from the team. "You should try rowing," my father says to me. Rowing is my father's sport. Every evening before dinner, the wheezy whir of his rowing machine whooshes through our home. "You'll be good at it," my father promises. "Rowing coaches usually make you run a lot too." I mope into Colgate's rowing office, sad about not running. The sadness soon passes. I row five-seat on the crew team during all four years of college, and under Title IX our sport is finally awarded varsity status. After graduation, I am invited to row with the U.S. National Lightweight Development team.

I finish my Escape From Alcatraz race a few hours before my father, coming in nineteenth in the professional women's category. There are Olympians and world champions in my field. It is my rookie year as a pro triathlete; I am no phenom, no podium topper, no household name. Just a hardworking athlete who wanted to see if it was possible to turn pro at the age of thirty. Turns out it's possible. Turns out it's worth it, even if no one ever knows your name. I tell my father the details of my race, how I felt good in the water and fast on the run, but that the bike felt strongest. I tell him I finished toward the back of my field, but not so bad for an old rookie.

"Like father, like daughter," my dad says proudly.

July 2001. Ironman Lake Placid. After three years of the short, local triathlon races I started doing in grad school, I sign up for my first Ironman event: 2.4-mile swim, 112-mile bike, 26.2-mile marathon. Family is there to cheer me on. Dad is mesmerized, but not so much by me. "Look at all the old farts out there!" he exclaims. "Maybe I could do a triathlon." This will be his tagline for the next three years. At sixty-six, he will sign up for his first race, the Westchester Triathlon in Rye, New York. I watch him shuffle across the finish line with his slanting lope of a stride and a huge smile on his face. I hand him Gatorade and cookies with tears streaming down my cheeks.

After our escape from Alcatraz, my father and I head to Ino's sushi restaurant in Mill Valley to celebrate our day of father–daughter athleticism. I live in Arizona; he lives in New York. Racing has kept us close in all regards. The pride of today's accomplishment is setting in, and I can literally see the experience of the day settle into his face. He has forgotten about the swim-course incident. Such is the beauty of athletic accomplishment. Eventually, all disappointments and glitches fade away and what's left is the true reminder of why we choose to be athletes: It makes us feel alive.

———

"You know how I want to die?" my dad says, mid California roll.

"I am definitely not having this conversation," I answer.

He ignores me. "No nursing home, no hospital. When I'm really old and start to lose it, I'm going to enter a triathlon. Then, as soon as I start fading on the run, I'm going to sprint. All out. Fast as I can. None of this steady, slow, shuffling, seventy-year-old stuff. I mean, I'm going to sprint until—"

"Dad—"

"—until my heart explodes! I mean, I have to go really, really fast, because I don't want to half-ass it and end up in a coma or on life support, you know? I'm gonna race the life right out of me right at the very end! Woo hoo! That's how you do it. You go out of this world doing what you love."

"But—"

"Don't worry, sweetheart, I'll sign a waiver."

"It won't work, Dad."

"And why is that?"

"I'd have to take your body off the course. That's outside assistance."

"No!"

"Yep. You'd be cheating."

He considers this for a moment. "Well, I guess it wouldn't be the first time."

June 2008. Vancouver, B.C. At the age of seventy-two, my father qualifies for a slot at the Triathlon World Championships. I am on the sidelines cheering him on, just as he was there to cheer me on a few months before during my Olympic trials in cycling. Although we're forty years apart in age and on opposite sides of the amateur/ professional divide, my father and I are strangely indistinguishable in the world of sports. We're two old athletes with the same goal: We just want to see how far we can go, how long we can cheat the expectations of age. As my dad comes shuffling around the corner of the run course, he gives me a high five and says, "This is my sprint lap. . . ." I simultaneously laugh and protest. His speed never changes. He lopes off toward the finish line. This is our routine.

KATHRYN BERTINE *is a professional cyclist and the author of two memoirs,* All the Sundays Yet to Come *and* As Good as Gold.

There's no end of ways in which one family member can become estranged from another. But as a tennis prodigy and a basketball legend find out, there's only one road back: hard work.

REACHING IN

⌇⌇

Tom Friend

She put her dad on a shelf and left him there for a quarter century. Just because the rest of the world was preoccupied with Julius Erving doesn't mean she's had to be. She says she has never Googled him, that she has never even heard of *The Fish That Saved Pittsburgh*. Instead, everything she's learned about the man has come second- or eighth-hand. She first found out he was her father when she was four, and she first started denying it when she was five. She'd say her father died in the war or that he was a sheik in Kuwait or that his name was "Ken." She didn't celebrate Father's Day, she celebrated *Grandfather's Day*. On dad–daughter nights at school, she'd show up with an uncle or a neighbor. On registration forms that required a father's name, she'd write "N/A" or "None of Your Business!" Through the years, Dr. J wasn't so much a secret as he was a figment of her imagination.

Until two months ago, when the phone rang . . .

UNCHARTED TERRITORY

There's no manual for this. There are no instructions for: Basketball icon meets female sportswriter, has extramarital affair, gets sportswriter pregnant, misses childbirth due to game against Pacers, asks for separate lives, reads about the child eighteen years later in the newspaper, has a broken heart, wishes for a way to reconcile, spends nine years thinking about it, can't pull the trigger.

There's no way to fix all that. Is there? There can't possibly be a happily ever after. Can there? There's no phone call that can heal everything. Correct?

Even if we retell the story, examine every nuance, revisit preschool and Wimbledon and the ESPYs and Troy, Alabama, the answer still has to be no. Or at least ninety percent no. Or eighty percent no. Or . . .

DOOMED FROM THE GET-GO

The couple—Julius Erving and Samantha Stevenson—had no chance from the start. He was a freelance dunker and she was a freelance writer, but other than that, they were from different planets. He was black, married, worshipped, and image-conscious. She was white, single, ostracized, and passionate about the truth. He helped pave the way for the NBA–ABA merger; she helped pave the way for women in the locker room. They met in the middle somewhere, circa 1976, and on December 15, 1980, she waited in a San Diego hospital for him to come kiss their newborn daughter.

"He was supposed to meet her, but he didn't show up," Samantha says. "He wasn't coming to rescue me, or be with me, so I moved on. I'm a big girl. The only thing I needed from him was his middle name: Winfield. I gave it to her because she was a part of him, because I wanted her to be tied to him."

The baby's full name was Alexandra Winfield Stevenson, and if Samantha had foreseen the drama ahead, she might have omitted his name from the birth certificate. But there it was, as plain as day, under *father of child:* Julius Winfield Erving II.

The early years were testy. From all accounts, Erving's wife, Turquoise, was fuming over her husband's infidelities and livid at Samantha. In 1977, two years before her affair with Erving, Samantha had ghost-written a piece with Turquoise about life as an NBA wife for *The New York Times,* and, naturally, Turquoise felt betrayed. So there was little hope of Julius ever flying Alexandra in for a visit. In fact, the terse agreement between the two parties, drawn up by lawyers, was for Samantha to live at least 200 miles away from Julius, keep the birth out of the news, receive a modest monthly stipend, and have sole custody. At the time, Julius was the reigning NBA MVP as a Philadelphia 76er, the good Doctor, and a paternity scandal—much less an interracial affair—could have been an image- and endorsement-killer. Samantha says she loved him and didn't want to be the cause of that. So she signed the contract, lived off his monthly checks, and stayed in her little corner of the world: La Jolla, California.

"For better or worse, the parties honored it," Erving says. "We thought it was in the best interest of Alexandra."

All mother and daughter had were each other—and a Schwinn bicycle to get them from Point A to B. Every morning, Samantha would put a crash helmet on her three-year-old toddler and pedal her to the grocery store, to the beach, and five miles to preschool. They were an odd couple riding down busy La Jolla Boulevard—a white mom and a mixed-race toddler—and one of Samantha's angrier days was when a curious preschool teacher asked Alexandra who her father was and what he did for a living.

Alexandra didn't have a clear answer for the questions, and when she came home in some distress, Samantha whipped out a book titled *The Legend of Dr. J.* She showed Alexandra a photo of a chiseled Erving, palming an ABA ball, in a New York Nets uniform, and she told her four-year-old: "This is your father. He's a great person, and he happens to be a basketball player. I'm your mom, and you live with me, but it's important for you to know he loves you."

She also explained his identity was "nobody's business," which is how an entire cover-up began. By kindergarten, Alexandra was drawing self-portraits of herself as white, and, by grade school, she was telling her mom, "The next time someone asks me who my father is, I'll say Robert Redford." Samantha suggested she think of someone else, to which Alexandra replied, "Sidney Poitier?"

She also began telling her mom she disliked her middle name, Winfield, and asked to switch it to Chloe or Zoe.

"What's wrong? Winfield sounds presidential," Samantha said.

"But I'm not running for president," Alexandra shot back.

Instead, she was running circles around the other kids in sports. As an infant, she'd done underwater somersaults in the swimming pool, and later she excelled in soccer, gymnastics, tennis, and ballet. Basketball she could take or leave. But then one day, at the age of eight, she came home from school with a flyer that said the recently retired Julius Erving was conducting a one-time-only clinic at the local gym. All the boys in her class were dying to meet him, and, out of curiosity, Alexandra asked Samantha if she, too, could go, if she could see her father, finally, in the flesh.

Samantha's reaction was "Are you sure?" And when Alexandra assured her she was, the wheels were set in motion. Samantha did not alert Julius, because they weren't communicating anyway. Instead, Alexandra showed up with one of Samantha's close girlfriends, who wrote ALEXANDRA STEVENSON in large block letters on a name tag . . . then stepped back to watch the fireworks.

At first, Julius didn't recognize Alexandra. He'd seen

photos of her—Samantha would send some to the 76er offices once or twice a year—but he didn't make the connection. What he did notice was a lanky, determined little girl, diving all over the court in her size 9 sneakers, and he chose her as one of the camp's top performers. Her prize was a personal autograph from him, and when he looked down and saw ALEXANDRA STEVENSON, Erving's exact baritone words—according to Samantha's friend, Geneva Kandel—were "Nice to meet you, Alexandra."

The little girl froze. She glared at Julius, said, "I don't want your autograph," and stomped away.

"I realized it was Alexandra, and it was quite embarrassing," Erving says. "I've replayed it a hundred times in my mind and thought about how it could've turned out differently, maybe if it had been set up a little better. It might be a wound that never heals for her. I was at the end of my career; a lot was going on. I was somewhat oblivious during that time."

Kandel actually remembers what she saw in Erving's eyes that day: tears. She remembers Turquoise, who was at the gym, fainting. And she remembers going back to retrieve the autographed basketball.

Alexandra brought the ball home that night and wouldn't let her mother see it or touch it. Instead, the little girl locked the bedroom door and examined her father's autograph for hours. She then placed the ball on the farthest reaches of her closet shelf, hid it behind her dolls, and firmly shut the closet door.

Never to look at it again.

FINDING HER OWN GAME

Basketball was now taboo to Alexandra. If her mom was watching a Lakers–Celtics game, circa 1988, the little girl would change the channel, or turn the TV completely off, always in a huff. Samantha would try showing her video highlights of Dr. J above the rim—above the square, for crying out loud—but Alexandra would roll her eyes. The little girl decided she already had a dad: *her mom.*

Samantha fretted over this and decided her daughter needed as many surrogate fathers as possible, which is where tennis came in. By age eight, Alexandra had already mastered every shot in the book—in pinafores handmade by Samantha's mother—and men's tennis coaches were fawning all over the kid.

Samantha began taking her to see Tracy Austin's coach, Robert Lansdorp—who told Samantha that Alexandra could be the next Margaret Court—and, at the age of ten, Alexandra was introduced to Pete Sampras's childhood coach, Pete Fischer. Samantha, who had been interviewing Fischer for a story, asked him to evaluate Alexandra's game, and when she served close to 100 mph, he predicted she could be No. 1 in the world someday.

Fischer, a pediatrician, was willing to coach Alexandra, but it would mean Samantha driving 240 miles, round-trip, from La Jolla to Los Angeles one day a week, and later three days a week. The Schwinn bicycle wouldn't cut it. They needed a reliable car, and guess who bought them a white Volvo station wagon.

"I wasn't in their life," Erving says, "but I was never a deadbeat dad. I didn't ignore them; I tried to support them."

The truth is, Erving had been raised by a single mother himself and had only laid eyes on his father, Julius Winfield Erving I, twice in his life. "And those couple occasions weren't really all that cool," Erving says.

He empathized with Alexandra's plight; she just didn't know it. She couldn't understand why, on her birthdays, there was never a card or a present. "Presents are big to me," she says. "I can't lie." She had no idea he felt his hands were tied by his wife and the agreement, no idea he was an attentive dad to four other children: Julius III, Jazmin, Cory, and an adopted son, Cheo. It was a shame, because both lawyers knew exactly how paternal Erving was and how maternal Samantha was. When Erving would visit Samantha's lawyer, he'd sometimes bring little Jazmin along to play. And when Samantha would negotiate with Erving's attorney, she'd always bring Alexandra in a Snugli. Erving's lawyer even held baby Alexandra in his arms. They weren't one big happy family, but they weren't coldhearted either. They were simply separated by legalese.

"With the lawyers involved, and Alexandra's mom and my wife, it put me in a very unusual position that there's no real preparation for," Erving says. "So I honored an agreement that if I look back on, would I do it again and do it the same way? I would prefer not to, but what's done is done.

"I've always had a parental love, knowing that I had a child out there, and I knew if there was ever a time she needed me, I would be there."

Regardless, Alexandra already had written him out of her life, and her philosophy on seeing him again became "better never than late." After that basketball clinic, she decided she'd forever belong to her mom and only her mom. She would sleep only in her mother's bed until she was seven, and, after that, they slept in adjacent twin beds in their one-bedroom apartment. Samantha felt it was crucial to almost spin a cocoon around her daughter. She'd hear, "Oh, are you babysitting?" when she'd take her out shopping, and she felt it was necessary to close ranks, to live only for her daughter.

So it was Samantha who chose not to date. It was Samantha who drove Alexandra the five hours back and forth to Fischer's tennis lessons. It was Samantha who brought her along on newspaper assignments, introducing her to top athletes such as Tony Gwynn and Steve Young. And when Alexandra wasn't allowed to be Dorothy in a school production of *The Wizard of Oz*—because of her skin color—it was Samantha who told her it was okay to be a green Wicked Witch.

Alexandra seemed content with her life, although someone would always ruin it and bring up the dad question. Lansdorp would joke: "Let's make a list of her potential dads—everyone in the tennis world wants to know who this brilliant athlete's father is!" Some people even guessed Wilt Chamberlain. Fischer, meanwhile, had noticed Alexandra's elongated hands, how she could palm a medium-sized basketball. Knowing Samantha's Philadelphia roots, he put two and two together and guessed Erving was the father. But he never mentioned it. Instead, he persuaded Alexandra to play a game of H-O-R-S-E, on a six-foot basket, and announced coyly, "My next shot is a Dr. J slam." Alexandra walked away.

The more she excelled in tennis, the more her secret was at risk. By the time she was twelve, Alexandra was already serving 100 mph and had practiced with Bobby Riggs, Ellsworth Vines, Don Budge, and Sampras. In high school, she'd blasted a serve so hard that her opponent walked off the court out of absolute fear. She and two other young girls—a certain Venus and Serena Williams—were the talk of amateur tennis, and when Richard Williams asked Fischer whether he'd coach his girls instead, Fischer answered, "No, I've got the better athlete."

That's what Samantha wanted fourteen-year-old Alexandra to understand—that she had superstar genetics. So, during a junior tennis tournament in Philadelphia, she took her daughter to the Julius Erving statue in front of the Spectrum. It was life-sized and bronze, and Alexandra, who had studied the Roman Empire, couldn't fathom why Julius Erving and Julius Caesar each had statues.

"What is so special about him?" she asked her mother.

THE VULTURES CIRCLE

The birth certificate was just sitting there in a San Diego hall of records, a fifty-cent phone call away.

Someone just had to think of it—perhaps an ambitious reporter—and it didn't help that Samantha might have tipped the whole thing off years before. Back in 1986, she had penned a diary for *World Tennis* magazine, and one particular excerpt seemed to have the vultures circling:

> What makes a champion? Red Smith once told me it's in the blood. I agree. A world-class athlete is born with the ability to be great. Alexandra has it. You DO know if your child's got it.

It doesn't seem like much, but a tennis writer from the Fort Lauderdale *Sun-Sentinel,* Charles Bricker, had heard the gossip, had read that diary, had seen the white mom carting around the mixed-race daughter, and by 1997 started snooping. Erving would eventually call it a "witch hunt," and, according to Samantha, it all began with a simple question to sixteen-year-old Alexandra at a national tournament:

"Who's your father?" Bricker asked.

"None of your business," Alexandra snapped. A year later, in March 1998, Bricker made the inevitable phone call to San Diego. He purchased the birth certificate, for a nominal amount, and saw Erving's name in plain sight.

"I never thought anyone would find it; I didn't think anyone would care," Samantha says. "I had lived my life quietly, and not once had I been asked for it. And I never second-guessed putting his name on it. He was her father, and I didn't want her to feel she was out in the world by herself. She needed to know two people were committed to her. Because I thought, one day, Julius would care."

The newspaper sat on the story, because—according to explanations given later by the *Sun-Sentinel*—Alexandra wasn't enough of a public figure yet. She was ranked only No. 120 in the world at the time, and Bricker hadn't even broached the subject with Alexandra and Samantha. But he was planning to do so, and in December of '98, at the Orange Bowl junior tournament, he took another run at the two of them.

"I know who your father is," Alexandra remembers Bricker saying. Which is when Samantha says she blew a gasket. "I said, 'Stay away from my daughter!' I probably used some bad language. He just stood there. I said, 'Don't you dare come near us again.' "

But it was only a matter of time, or a matter of Alexandra hitting the big time. She skipped the 1999 French Open the following May so she could go to her prom, graduate, and portray cheerleader Patty Simcox in her high school's presentation of *Grease*. But she wasn't going to miss Wimbledon that June. She had to qualify first, in Roehampton, England, and with her first serve hitting close to 125 mph and her second serve skidding along at 108, she was made for the grass. Before long, she was in the third round of the main draw, recording an upset of eleventh-seeded Julie Halard-Decugis. The British crowd adored her classic one-hand backhand and her postmatch curtsies and serenaded her with a standing ovation. She felt like she was back at La Jolla Country Day School, channeling Sandra Dee. She was barely showing anxiety, which was more than Dr. J could say.

Back in Florida, where Erving was a senior vice president for the Orlando Magic, he says he was evading phone calls from Bricker. Julius hadn't been watching Wimbledon, but he'd seen in the newspaper that Alexandra was torching her opponents, and he sensed the *Sun-Sentinel* was ready to move with the story.

"First of all, in talking to someone I don't know, it's none of their business," Erving says. "And I wouldn't corroborate, cooperate, or confirm what his findings were because, as I said, I thought it was a witch hunt, and I really wasn't properly approached by someone who I knew and could trust."

Back in London, Samantha was still reveling in the victory over Halard-Decugis when Frank Deford, her sportswriter friend, alerted her of the latest pressroom rumor: Someone had scored Alexandra's birth certificate. The British tabloids would've hounded Alexandra to no end if that went public, and Deford's advice, according to Samantha, was to distract the media. So Samantha did a "walkabout" with the tabs, calling the tennis circuit an "evil place," talking about racism on the tour and proclaiming she wanted her daughter to marry a man. The tabloids implied she was bashing lesbians on the tour, and the headlines screamed: GET

YOUR FILTHY HANDS OFF MY DAUGHTER. Duplicitous or not, she says she was simply putting her daughter first. And mission accomplished: Good ol' Samantha was now on the front page—not Alexandra.

"Who cared what Charlie Bricker knew?" Samantha says. "Nobody cared about that. They only cared about the lesbians."

The Stevensons were the rage of Wimbledon. Nike might have dropped Alexandra as a client before the tournament, but now Phil Knight had personally flown in to re-sign her. Here was the next great American player, and after she recorded a scintillating fourth-round, three-set victory over Lisa Raymond, she was the favorite in her quarterfinal match against fellow qualifier Jelena Dokic. One problem: Bricker's story was going public.

The night before the Dokic match, Samantha was told the *Sun-Sentinel* story would move on the AP wires in the morning. She spoke with her lawyer, coached Alexandra on what to say, and then awoke to another bombshell: Erving had denied it.

Julius claims he just didn't corroborate it, but Alexandra was aghast. "I just thought that was dumb," she says. "Maybe he got blindsided. I mean, I don't know what was going on in his life at the time. Maybe it got thrown in his face like it got thrown in mine. Maybe he panicked."

Alexandra somehow defeated Dokic in a rain-delayed match, becoming the first woman qualifier ever to reach the Wimbledon semis. But, in her ninth match of the fortnight, a drained Alexandra fell to Lindsay

Davenport 6–1, 6–1. By then, Erving had come clean and admitted, in a statement, that Alexandra was indeed his flesh and blood. Privately, Julius was relieved the secret was out, that "another journey was about to begin," and, in his statement, he asked people to give Alexandra her space at this difficult time. But the truth was, she'd never have space again.

When her flight landed in Boston, she was greeted with raucous applause in the terminal. Airport workers and baggage clerks howled, "Dr. J's daughter!" She'd never heard those words in public before, not in all her eighteen years. Now she finally knew the answer to the question she'd asked at the statue: *What was so special about her dad?* Everybody loved him, which meant everybody adored her.

She waited for his call, but a torn Erving was second-guessing what to do. He'd seen Alexandra's post Wimbledon quote—"He didn't change my diapers, my mom did." He'd read that she didn't like being called African American, that she crumpled up newspapers that referred to her as Dr. J's kid, that she only considered herself a Stevenson. He assumed she was sending him a message.

"With her interviews and her feelings about not having a father and not having brothers and sisters, I thought [contacting] her would be a nightmare," he says. "I really thought she tuned out the Ervings as really existing. The Ervings weren't only at a distance, the Ervings didn't exist."

Reality was, she didn't have anything figured out at eighteen, other than she wanted a hot-pink tennis racket. "Why didn't I call him? Because I thought he should call me," Alexandra says. "He's the grown-up. But I just got over it and figured, 'Oh, well, he'll never call.' So you move on. And then I just got annoyed at airports."

It got to the point that whenever she'd hear, "Hey, Dr. J's daughter," at the airport, she'd deny it. She'd say, "No, I'm not." They'd see her rackets and ask, "Are you sure?" And she'd answer, "Yeah, I'm sure." She was stoic on the outside, but there were obviously layers of hurt inside. Later that summer, Alexandra went to visit her friends from La Jolla, the Kandels. They were a traditional family, with a father and mother, brothers and sisters, pillow fights, bunk beds, and chores. It struck her that somewhere out there, she had a family too.

So, for the first time since Wimbledon, for the first time since the Bricker story, Alexandra fell to her knees and sobbed.

LOSING HER WAY

Who was going to blink first?

Not the tennis player, because she had wins and losses—mainly losses—to worry about. In Alexandra's first thirty-two tournaments following Wimbledon, her first thirty-two tournaments as a celebrity's kid, she lost in the first round *twenty times*. And after each loss, the media still wanted her in the interview room.

She quickly learned the routine. They'd start off lobbing softball questions, until some writer with a nervous tic would ask, "Have you contacted your father? Has your father contacted you?"

Her standard answer became "No, the father ship hasn't landed yet"—because she felt it was a silly question that deserved a silly answer. But, deep down, it wasn't amusing. Her mother had just lost her writing contract with *The New York Times* for becoming *the* story at Wimbledon. And, in all of these first-round matches, the bull's-eye was on Alexandra. She'd gone from the hunter to the hunted, from *Grease* to *Girl, Interrupted*. After a first-round loss at the Australian Open, early in 2000, she was MIA for forty-five minutes, weeping in a nearby garage. It dawned on her: If she hadn't starred at Wimbledon and turned pro, she'd have been at UCLA or Stanford or Harvard, and Bricker wouldn't have had a reason to blow her cover. But instead she was a Top 50 player . . . and a wreck.

"At Wimbledon, I was under the radar as myself," Alexandra says. "After Wimbledon, everyone expected me to go win Grand Slams and tournaments right way. Plus, I had the whole father issue. Coaches kept saying, 'Oh, it's mental.' Well, it probably was mental! Because I'm getting interviewed about a father I didn't know every time."

Her surrogate dad, Fischer, wasn't there to save her either. Shockingly, he'd been charged with child molestation prior to Wimbledon—a head-turner for Alexandra, who said she had never felt threatened by him. He eventually pleaded guilty and accepted a six-year prison sentence, leaving Alexandra alone with her mother and trying to master the pro tour. They'd hire their coaches du jour—Nick Bollettieri included—but it was ultimately up to the kid to figure out how to win.

To her credit, she buckled down. By the end of 2002, she had risen to No. 18 in the world, an absolute budding star. She'd played brilliant matches against all the huge names—including consecutive wins over No. 1 Jennifer Capriati—and simply needed to mix in some finesse with all that power. Life was just better. She bought a condo in Florida, decorated it in pink. But her mom wouldn't let her buy a car. They still had the trusty white Volvo station wagon, the one Julius bought them when she was eleven, and, even though it had 250,000 miles on it, Samantha saw it almost as a family heirloom.

"That car was his present to her," Samantha says. "It was symbolic, something connected to him. Like when I gave her his middle name. I told her, 'You take care of it, you don't just throw things away.' It had meaning; it was a symbol of her hard work."

Deep down, Samantha must've been wishing for some father–daughter reconciliation, because about twice a year she'd have a recurring dream, where Julius would magically appear on a basketball court, showing Alexandra how to play hoops. They'd be smiling and joking—until Samantha would wake up in a cold sweat.

In real time, though, Julius was dealing with a nightmare. In the spring of 2000, just months after Wimbledon, his son Cory went missing, the same Cory who was born less than six months after Alexandra. The boy had always been a lost soul, afflicted with attention deficit disorder and sucked in by cocaine. He'd been to rehab and, in 1998, was charged with burglarizing a car and loitering and prowling, charges that were later dropped. But he'd also been the one son with some Dr. J in him, the one son who was six-foot-four and able to reverse-dunk. And, at age nineteen, Cory was finally taking pride in that. He found a job at a restaurant and was playing a lot of hoops at the local blacktop. He seemed to be stable until, one day, he never showed up for a barbecue. He was missing for forty days, and, during that horrible stretch, Erving went on *Larry King Live* to plead for help. King asked, on the air, whether Alexandra had been in touch, and he said no. So that was two daggers in Julius's heart.

He'd often think about Alexandra—"Part of me always missed her, missed not having her around," he says—but when Cory eventually was found dead, having accidentally driven his car into a pond and drowned, the drama was almost too much to take. Erving's marriage to Turquoise was eroding and, adding to the mayhem, Julius had just become the father of a newborn son, Jules, with another woman, Dorýs Madden. He describes that time in his life as "day to day," and he wasn't entirely certain where Alexandra fit in.

But after he and Turquoise divorced, reaching out to Alexandra seemed more plausible. He'd been following her career; he'd even talked to John McEnroe about her. He'd know when she was in Philly or Florida or California. Some of his close friends urged him to get on a plane, and it was eventually broached to Samantha, through an intermediary, that Erving might like to meet Alexandra backstage at the 2004 ESPYs. Alexandra was going to be there with Venus and Serena, but Samantha thought a backstage reunion would be a logistical disaster, not to mention impersonal. She balked at it, and Erving, at the same time, had his own second thoughts as well.

"I wanted to meet her and see her, and I played it out a lot of times in my mind how it would go, the hits I would have to take and the surprise factor," Erving says. "But then it kept falling from the list of priorities for me, and I just didn't get it done. It's no excuse. I had pretty much grown accustomed to not having her as part of my life, so I didn't know what I was missing. And she didn't have tremendous need for a father or a father figure to suddenly come into her life and play a dominant role or even a small role. So I was okay with that as long as she was okay."

But she wasn't okay—not her shoulder, anyway. At the Australian Open in January 2003, she felt an electrical shock in her rotator cuff, and in a match at Amelia Island that spring, the shock spread to her wrist. By July, the diagnosis was a torn right labrum and, although she tried playing through it, her ranking was dropping like an anvil.

In September 2004, Dr. James Andrews performed labrum surgery, and since NFL quarterbacks regularly came back even stronger from that operation, Andrews figured she'd be her old self in 2005. But tennis isn't quarterbacking; it's incessant serving and ball-striking. Alexandra's arm was constantly fatigued, and by August 2005, she'd fallen to a personal low of No. 909 in the world. In 2006, Samantha put her on a quasi–pitch count, meaning she'd retire from any match if her arm tired. Tournament directors complained about it and stopped offering wild-card entries into main draws. Alexandra's ranking fluctuated between 400 and the upper 600s that year, and Andrews, at one point, thought she might need a second surgery. Her agent was gone, Nike was gone, and her cash flow took a hit. Samantha, who was now Alexandra's full-time manager, reluctantly had to borrow money from friends.

During 2006, 2007, and 2008, Alexandra had no choice but to play regularly on the Challenger tour, the minor leagues, in cities such as Ashland, Kentucky, and Rockford, Illinois, where a loss in the first round would net her $75. She and Samantha shared meals at restaurants or cooked chicken in their low-budget hotel suites. Much of their life savings had been exhausted on trainers and practice partners and travel and hotels—it can cost about $3,000 a week to play tournaments—and they began asking tournament directors for housing. But several directors said no, that foreign players get first dibs. So Samantha was forced to solicit local country clubs, looking for members with a guest room.

Her circumstances became so dire that sometimes Alexandra could only afford to bring one freshly strung racket onto the court; gut strings were too expensive. She couldn't afford prematch hitting partners, either, so sometimes she'd warm up against a backboard. A friend, Roman Prokus, was still customizing her rackets, but she owned only six-month-old hard-court shoes. So when she went south to play clay-court tournaments in the Carolinas to try to drum up enough points to reach the 2008 Wimbledon qualifying, she carved grooves in her hard-court sneakers with a penknife—anything to improve her footing.

Samantha would quote Vince Lombardi or Tom Landry to Alexandra, to keep her spirits up. "Well, I didn't have any Julius quotes," she says. But then something happened—Alexandra began playing more tactical clay-court tennis, slicing her backhand, spinning in more serves. She'd reinvented herself as a finesse player and reached the main draw of a main WTA event in Charleston, South Carolina, jumping up from 377th in the world to 258th, earning enough points to go to Wimbledon qualifying. She also met a man there, a local twenty-five-year-old teaching pro. They began to date, and she took him with her to Wimbledon.

She hadn't been this excited to be in London since '99—and she carried around a picture of the Wimbledon championship plate while she trained. But she slipped on the grass in an early qualifying match, injured her hip, and strained her shoulder compensating. Devastated, she wept for four days, and when she returned to the States, she removed all her Wimbledon memorabilia from her house. It was back to the minor leagues at the age of twenty-seven, where the tournament directors were pointing her to the back courts and where the other players hated her because she still stole all their headlines. It wasn't her fault camera crews were coming to see only her, or that newspapers put her above the fold. It was all about who her father was. So she quit talking to the media, and in a late-September match in Troy, Alabama, while trying to play with her strained shoulder, while dealing with boyfriend troubles, she lost it.

"Because of all my emotions and all this hatred toward me—people wanting me to fail—I just took it all out on the court," she says. "So I threw my racket, and I never throw my racket. And then I said 'f——,' and I never cuss. I'd say, 'I hate this f——ing sport. I'm done with this. I quit.' And then I had a primal scream that came from nowhere."

She returned to Birmingham that October so physical therapist Kevin Wilk could treat her mild shoulder strain, and she and Samantha happened to bump into former pro golfer Jerry Pate, a good friend of Erving who'd been rehabbing his own injury. In the past, Pate had bragged how good a fellow Julius was, and they'd said, "Then why won't he call?!!" But Alexandra was desperate for help now, on pace to earn only $35,000 for the year. She needed someone who could find her sponsors, someone who had contacts. And Julius had to have contacts. He'd been hamming it up in Dr Pepper commercials. He was loved all over the world. They'd heard and seen it. They'd lived it. So they asked Pate for her father's phone number.

"It was time. I didn't want her to turn thirty and not know her father," Samantha says. "We went through the first eighteen years holding a secret, and we went through the last nine years keeping people away from her. Enough is enough. She should know her father."

She asked Alexandra to call him, but Alexandra was ambivalent. So Samantha dialed him instead, reached his voice mail, paused . . . and let it fly: "Hello, Julius, this is Samantha twenty-seven years later. We were supposed to talk on December fifteenth, 1980, but you never showed up. But since I've got your phone number now, I thought you might like to meet that person you were supposed to meet twenty-seven years ago. Please call me back."

He never returned the call. Not that day, not the next five days. So, before her next tournament in Quebec City on October 28, Alexandra called. It went straight to voice mail again, so she paused, then got right to it: "Hello, Julius, this is Alexandra. I believe my mother called you last week, and we've never heard back from you. Maybe you've been traveling or you've lost the number. Can you please call back?"

At the time, they thought, fat chance, and went to bed. But the next morning, Alexandra awoke to a voice mail from a man with a deep voice:

"Hello, Alexandra, this is your father calling. Thank you for the phone call. Would you please call me back?"

She had a match to play that day, which was her convenient excuse not to call him back. The whole scenario had rattled her. What would they talk about? Was this real? What's with that voice? By the time she and her mother returned from the match, he'd left four more voice messages. He was invisible for twenty-seven years, and now he's stalking her? They climbed into bed, and the lights had barely been out when the phone rang again at eleven p.m.

Samantha answered, and Erving, mistaking her for his daughter, said it again: "Hi, Alexandra, this is your father."

"Who?" Samantha asked, half asleep. But she quickly gained her bearings, said, "Ooooooh, hold on," and literally threw the phone to Alexandra.

So Erving said it one more time: "Hi, Alexandra. This . . . is . . . your . . . father."

"Hello, Julius," she said.

TOGETHER AGAIN . . . FOR THE FIRST TIME

One phone call can't fix the world, but it can thaw it a little.

The minute father and daughter started talking, there were sparks . . . in a good way. His first question was "How are you?" and she answered, "I just lost a match today; I'm not feeling too great." He asked her what happened, and when she told him about her shoulder soreness, he mentioned he used to ice both his knees after every 76ers game. He asked her what her career ambitions were, and she almost started crying. If only he knew about Troy and the minor leagues. She told him she still wanted to be No. 1 in the world, and that no one believed in her, and he said he'd always wanted to be No. 1, too, that he always wanted to trash the Celtics, and that no one believed in him coming out of UMass.

He told her she had a good seven years left, and she said, "I agree, but it takes money, and I don't have it. And that's one of the reasons I called you, because I need financial support. And I hate asking for help, but I need help."

He told her he'd do everything in his power to find her sponsors but wanted to meet her first. She giggled, and that's what he noticed first—that she sounded like a schoolgirl, a pleasant, exuberant schoolgirl. He told her he owned and operated a golf club in Atlanta, and that he'd like her to see it, that he'd been thinking about putting in some tennis courts. Maybe she could give him advice.

She told him she was already planning to be in nearby Birmingham that week to see Wilk, and so they made a date for Halloween day.

"Well, I'm looking forward to meeting you," Erving said.

"Me too," Alexandra said. "And you know why? Because for nine years, I've been going through airports hearing, 'There's Dr. J's kid.' And now I finally get to meet Dr. J."

He laughed his loudest laugh and hung up the phone, a forty-minute phone call that had a stunned Samantha saying, "It was as if they knew each other their whole lives."

But it was hardly a fleeting moment. He called the next day to see whether she'd made her flight to Birmingham, if she'd arrived safely. He sounded like an overprotective papa, and he still started every message with "Hi, Alexandra, this is your father." She was flattered, but she still complained to her mom, "Can he just say 'Julius'?"

Erving was simply ready for this. He was fifty-eight, pushing sixty. He could think of three times in the previous two years when he'd nearly invited her to events—a housewarming, a family reunion, and a New Year's party. But he'd preferred she make the first move, and now that she had, he wasn't letting go.

"Why did this happen now? It doesn't matter," he says. "I'm not curious as to why. I'm not suspicious. I'm not worried about this great ulterior motive that I'm going to help her get back into the world of tennis, and then she's going to kick me to the curb or whatever. I'm okay. I'd be remiss to think she won't have wounds. I'm prepared. I've been around a long time. I'm an old dog and I'm prepared."

On Halloween morning, she arrived at the golf club and asked the bartender where "Julius" was. She wasn't going to ask for "Dad" or "Father." It was Julius and only Julius. Just a year before, one of her tennis friends had given her a Dr. J DVD, and she'd thrown it out. So this was a leap for her.

He emerged from his office and gave her a bear hug. He couldn't take his eyes off her. He thought she looked like his mother and one of his sisters, neither of whom is still alive, and got emotional. He noticed her chestnut eyes and her long hands. They were his hands. Samantha had noticed their identical hands from the first sonogram of Alexandra in her womb. And when Erving was done admiring her, he invited her into a private room.

His first line was "Well, I only thought this would happen at my funeral, all seven of my children in the same area, and Cory, of course, in spirit."

She said, "Yes, I'm sorry about Cory," and he thanked her and began talking about his family as if she knew his life story. She stopped him and told him she knew nothing, that she'd never Googled him, that she "wasn't a computer geek." He said, "Oh, you're like an old soul. You're old school, I like that." So he gave her the rundown. There were Jazmin, Julius, and Cheo from his marriage to Turquoise, and ten-year-old Jules, seven-year-old Justin, and baby Julietta from his current relationship with Dorýs. Six half brothers and sisters, in one fell swoop.

She asked him why he had waited twenty-seven years to call—the money question—and she says he answered: "Well, it was a bad situation. My wife wouldn't let me contact you. She was devastated by the affair, but that's not an excuse. We worked everything out through the lawyers, and that's how it was forever." She nodded and didn't ask a follow-up. He was prepared to be peppered, but she let it drop.

"She wasn't walking around with a chip on her shoulder," he says. "What started as a conversation flowed into a sort of camaraderie, where it became 'What are we going to do later?' instead of saying good-bye. We started at midday and kept going for hours, and there's something to be said for that."

He took her back to his condo, where she bonded with Dorýs and their kids. Alexandra was enthralled at how affectionate Erving was with the children, how they nestled in his lap. They later went to dinner, and while Julius was in the restroom, a waiter recognized Alexandra and gushed all over her. The chef even personally brought out Alexandra's food. Dorýs thought they all had a crush on her, but, no, that's just how it was to be Dr. J's celebrity tennis daughter. All over the world.

At the tail end of the evening, seven hours later, she and Julius sat alone in his car, and he brought up her earlier question about why he hadn't called in twenty-seven years. He told her it was because she'd been well cared for by her mom, and that if she hadn't been, he would've come to rescue her. His eyes were red, and he seemed close to breaking down. He told her, "I trust you, and I need you to try to trust me." She asked him again about rounding up sponsors, and that almost had her in tears too. She told him creditors were always calling her, saying, "We know who your father is—pay up." He assured her he'd try to help because he knew what it was like to be an athlete, the desire to go out on your own terms.

"It's not how you enter your sport, it's how you exit," her father said. She adored that line.

She finally had her Dr. J quote.

"HELP ME FIND A WAY TO CALL YOU DAD"

He wasn't going to wait another twenty-seven years . . . or even another twenty-four hours.

The next day, he invited Alexandra and Samantha to Justin's birthday party, then was thrilled to hear they had accepted. He had gone to bed the previous night overwhelmed. Icons are people, too, and Erving considered it a "life-changing event" to meet his long-lost daughter.

"Meeting her that day for me ranks up there, really, with the NBA championship, the ABA championships, the induction into the Hall of Fame," he says. "I wasn't there when she was born, but that's right up there with the birth of your child—and this one is a rebirth."

Inviting Samantha into his inner circle was a little more perplexing. Their affair had ended when she'd become pregnant with Alexandra, and they had last spoken a few days before Alexandra was born. And the last time they'd laid eyes on each other, he was in a limo about to have his DNA tested—to see whether he was truly Alexandra's father—and she was on a Philadelphia sidewalk after her own DNA test. So it'd been a long time, and when she stopped in to see him at the golf club on November 1, she shook his hand and said, "Nice to see you again."

"It's *really* nice to see you," Erving responded.

There was a mutual respect all around. Dorýs conversed with Samantha; Samantha chatted up Jazmin; and the younger kids piled on to Alexandra. At one point, Julius sauntered over to sit alone with Alexandra and Samantha, wanting to hear more about his daughter's life. She told him she'd graduated from the University of Colorado, online, in six and a half years, finishing on the dean's list. She told him she'd lugged textbooks all over Europe. He then asked to hear every detail of the '99 Wimbledon fortnight. The two women happily recounted every match . . . Alexandra's curtsies . . . Samantha's controversial comments . . . Phil Knight flying in. Erving was riveted. He asked why Bricker had exposed their story, and no one had an answer for him. Samantha said, "We kept it secret for eighteen years, and we would've kept it longer. But who knew she'd be so talented?"

"Thank God she was," he said. "Thank God."

By day's end, the seven children—Alexandra included—posed for a picture with Julius, then Alexandra and her mom were off to the airport. As usual, someone said, "There's Dr. J's daughter"—and wasn't that the truth.

Back home, Alexandra sat down and crafted letters to each of her brothers and sisters, plus one to her father:

> Dear Julius,
> It's going to be really difficult for me to find a way to call you Dad. So you're going to have to help me with that. But I wanted to write this letter to thank you for giving me the most amazing moment of meeting you, and watching you talk to my mother.
> Alexandra

He wrote her back—although he preferred text messages—and one of his responses was:

> Dearest Alexandra,
> For a 27-year-old girl, you've had many disappointments and much pain in your life, more than anyone I know at your age. I understand.
> Love, Dad

Two weeks later, Alexandra and Samantha flew again to Atlanta, where Alexandra actually agreed to get on a basketball court with her father, agreed to play the sport she used to hate. It was Samantha's recurring dream come true, and Julius taught Alexandra how to shoot and how to dribble with her head up. The fundamentals. Alexandra coaxed him onto a tennis court and returned the favor. He wasn't half bad hitting from the baseline. He also spent an afternoon watching her train and sprint—"She runs like I did," he says—and, when she was done, he hugged her, patted her shoulder . . . and felt her pull away.

"For him to hug me, that's just weird to me—because I've never had that male, dad figure in my life," she says.

"Well," Erving says, "we've lost so much time you've just got to lay it out there. When I see her, I want to hug her, hold her. It's important to show love and affection, because I don't want to send any mixed messages, and I'm not a 'sometimey' person.

"But I did sense a hesitancy on her part. I don't expect her to just jump right in, hook, line, and sinker. There have to be wounds."

There's no way he can possibly fix them. Is there? There can't possibly be a happily ever after. Can there? There's no phone call that could heal everything. Correct?

The answer had to be no. Or forty percent no. Or twenty percent no. Or . . .

ALEXANDRA "MOMENTS" FOREVER

Back at her Los Angeles condo, there was a certain hop in Alexandra's step. Her shoulder was sound again, as sound as it had been since surgery, and former Olympic gold medalist Sherri Howard was training her body, legs, and soul. Pete Fischer, out of prison, was asking to work on her serve again, and Robert Lansdorp already had tuned up her ground strokes. Now ranked No. 212 in the world, she had put her original team back together, plus one slight addition: Dr. J.

He's already making sure, through his contacts, that she has sufficient funds to fly to Australia for 2009 Australian Open qualifying, and even though he can't be there, he hopes to be courtside at this summer's U.S. Open. He used to be the talk of Rucker Park; why not Flushing Meadow?

Alexandra had done a lot of thinking about him while she was home and said to herself, "It's not a movie. He wasn't going to swoop in like a fairy tale." But she also remembered something he said in Atlanta, that the two of them were stronger together than apart. So she sent him this text about three weeks ago:

> Hi. I've decided that I'm going to send you an Alexandra fact, an Alexandra favorite, and an Alexandra moment for the rest of your life until the day you die. I hope you don't mind, but I thought you should get to know me. Today's fact: I love the color pink . . . but I like to wear black and tan.

His response:

> Alexandra,
> I enjoyed your special message today. It means a lot to know you've committed to being in my life. I will be in yours, as well. . . . You have captured my

imagination with Alexandra moments, and I want to at least offer you father's hugs, daddy's kisses, and parent support forever. I hope you are OK today and always.

Love, Dad

She saved his messages; their relationship clearly was evolving. She told him she had broken up with the tennis pro from Charleston, and he asked for the guy's phone number so he could give him a good talking-to. It was such a fatherly thing to do. On another day, she signed a text: "Your daughter, Alexandra," and "It jumped off the phone" to him, Erving said. He wondered if this was the breakthrough, if deep down she might soon be ready to call him Dad.

Who knew? About that same time, Samantha began cleaning out their garage, as part of getting ready for Australia. She backed out the white Volvo station wagon (still going strong) and started sorting through drawers. She then stumbled onto something archaic, something stunning—the basketball Erving had autographed twenty years before for Alexandra, the one she'd hidden away on a shelf in her old bedroom closet.

Samantha had never looked at the ball up close before and seen Erving's signature. Then she squinted . . . and found something else sketched there.

It turns out that on that day, twenty years before, little Alexandra had sat in her room and written two more names on that basketball:

Julius ♥ and Alexandra ♥

That had been the *other* quarter-century secret:
She'd always missed him.

TOM FRIEND *is a senior writer at ESPN.com and* ESPN
The Magazine *and also an on-air reporter for ESPN.
He has previously worked for* The New York Times,
The National Sports Daily, The Washington Post, *the*
Los Angeles Times, *the* San Jose Mercury News, *and*
The Kansas City Star. *He has coauthored two books:*
Educating Dexter, *the autobiography of Dexter Manley,
and* Jack of All Trades, *the autobiography of Jack Mc-
Keon. A graduate of the University of Missouri, he has
been published in the Best American Sports Writing se-
ries and was named by* Men's Journal *one of America's
Top 20 sportswriters. He lives in Southern California
with his wife and two children.*

The poems on the following pages were written by an
English teacher at Kettle Falls (Washington) High School,
Lynn Rigney Schott. She is the daughter of Bill "Specs"
Rigney, an All Star infielder for the New York Giants in the
late 1940s and early '50s, who went on to manage in
the majors for eighteen seasons. He died in 2001.

PURE POETRY

≈≈≈

Lynn Rigney Schott

Spring Training

The last of the birds has returned
the bluebird, shy and flashy.
The bees carry fat baskets of pollen
from the alders around the pond.
The wasps in the attic venture downstairs,
where they congregate on warm windowpanes.
Every few days it rains.

This is my thirty-fifth spring;
still I am a novice at my work,
confused and frightened and angry.
Unlike me, the buds do not hesitate,
the hills are confident they will be
perfectly reflected
in the glass of the river.

I oiled my glove yesterday.
Half the season is over.
When will I be ready?

On my desk sits a black-and-white postcard picture
of my father—skinny, determined,
in a New York Giants uniform—
ears protruding, eyes riveted.
Handsome, single-minded, he looks ready.

Thirty-five years of warmups.
Like glancing down at the scorecard
in your lap for half a second
and when you look up it's done—
a long fly ball, moonlike,
into the night
over the fence,
way out of reach.

How It Was at Second
for my father

"He tore it off like a chicken wing—see?
(a garland of scar around the thumb) cleats
high as Cobb's and me hanging in, skinny
as ever, ready to turn two, my meat
hand dangling like bait before those mean teeth.
As they carried me off the field he called,

'Hey, Four-eyes! What do you think about that?'
'Maybe the good Lord'll pick up the ball—
who knows? It's a long season on the grass,
you bastard.' In the end, in Boston, God
disguised as Musial lined a final blast
off his nose. I wired him a knowing nod."

He smiled, remembering to his daughter
the kick and the smirk of Enos Slaughter.

Souvenirs
to my daughter, born February 6, Babe Ruth's birthday

In 1928 my grandfather gave a baseball
signed by Babe Ruth
to my father, who was ten.
Such balls travelled around by the dozen
in the Babe's suitcase and arrived
eventually in many small hands.
Dad grew up on Frisbie Street in Oakland
and there were never enough baseballs
in the neighborhood, so this one became
a game ball, not a collector's item.
By the end of a season it was so scuffed
up that the autograph just wore off
the horsehide, disappearing under so many
groundballs, so many slaps of the bat.
But all those pitches, those double-play
balls, those afternoons in the sand lot
never faded, only sharpened
his reflexes and his ambition and his boyish
love of this game that became the indelible
signature written all over my father's life.

A Bird in the Hand

When my father tells a story
his hands do much of the talking.
Like a proper shortstop he has large hands,
"soft" hands to be sure, and they move
with the rhythm of the narrative
the bassline beneath the melody—
sweeping, rolling, pointing, extending—
crescendo, allegro, staccato, ritardando.
He might be holding an invisible ball
or socking an invisible glove, miming
the scoop of a double play ball and the toss to second,
waving for the left-hander out of the bullpen.

Sometimes I think of birds—
a flurry of swallows swooping through
the open barn in early spring,
or the geese that flew over yesterday
right on time for the playoffs,
honking in a muted sort of mumble
like a restless crowd,
their wings feeling the weight of the fall air
and responding with a dull riffle of feathers
like fingers through the dust of the infield.
Or it might be a flock of pigeons
landing on the maze of cables
along the foul line at the old Coliseum.

Yes, hands like birds cutting through summer light
over the outfield, out to the bleachers.
Hands and words that will fly, fly away!
giving wing to this life,
these stories stitched in vibrant seams
outside the gravity of books
binding imagination and history and old friends
who listen with nothing but time on our hands,
each syllable lifted on a breeze
over one more bright diamond.

On Deck

At dawn we drive to the hospital,
Mt. Diablo looming drowsy in the autumn light,
the morning a yawn we try to stifle, like doubt.
Your empty stomach is full of a hollow
courage and the thing with feathers.
The weather? The wind is blowing out to right.

Now the nurse draws the drape around
our small space here in the dugout of
this great stadium to science and you
change into your uniform: not the old wool
baggies, the cleats, the black cap with the leggy
orange NY entwined on the front. This morning
it's the light-blue cotton gown, the rubber-soled
booties, the gauzy gray beret. And your pale legs,
pale and blue, look cold to me so I pull
the blanket up to cover them. Somewhere
the shortstop turns to cover second.

The room is bright and we wait. We don't
agree with those who say the game is too slow.
You read the sports page, I work a crossword.
Others are also in uniform—a woman with a torn
Achilles' tendon, a man with a back injury—
as the pre-op room pulses with its strange efficiency,
its otherworldly light, its green figures
with clipboards. In the sterile, silver warmth
silently I bless them all. Then we stand for
the national anthem: It's time to play ball.

You roll over and the nurse paints
your flank with long streaks of rusty Betadine.
She locates a vein on the back of your hand
and starts the IV. The metal stand
hovers at your shoulder like a rookie
after your spot in the lineup.

The anesthesiologist arrives—a Harvard man,
a fan. He explains his particular brand of
mischief, then settles in for a chat. As the drugs
invite you to forget where you are (which park? which
league?), to postpone pain (what was it Sparky said?
a little pain doesn't hurt . . .) you drift deep into
the infield and he grills you about the '51 pennant race.

I adjust the pillows at your back thinking
you look like a king giving audience to
some foreign diplomat, or an aging artist
(it's the beret) being interviewed for public TV;
I'm even reminded of John and Yoko and the peace
vigil from bed. But best of all, as you go
under, I get to hear once again about

Brooklyn and New York, the late race, the blazing
comeback as you gained 13½ games on the Dodgers
the last weeks of August, 39-and-8 down the stretch,
    you won
16 straight, then the third game of the playoff and
Stanky's quip in the fifth that Newk was "losing it" and
then you're pinch hitting to lead off the eighth, it's 4–1

and Newk's throwing rockets so you look over at
  Stanky and
your raised eyebrows say *oh yeah?* and Newk strikes
you out on three pitches and strikes out the side
but no matter because Dark and Mueller single
in the ninth and Lockman doubles and Bobby hits
the home run off Branca and Russ Hodges' voice
still carries this claim to history the way
the deep veins of baseball are claiming the map of
your body, the mind's motherlode framing the anatomy
of all the innings and years and the wind-filled flags
flying over the scoreboard and the scorecard that names
each moment in an illumination of small squares . . .

I can't believe the anesthetic isn't muddling
your memory or your syntax or your stats.
The story is perfect, precise, play-by-play, while
the rest of us in the stands would have trouble
counting balls and strikes or finding our seats.

Then all at once I am weak with your ordeal
and I want to go to bat for you here
in this bright circle of weird light, here
late in the game, it's the bottom of the ninth.

LYNN RIGNEY SCHOTT *lives on a small farm near the
Columbia River. Her husband, Stephen, is a beekeeper,
and they have two daughters. Her work has appeared
in* The New Yorker, Idaho English Journal, CutBank,
Elysian Fields Quarterly, *as well as* The Fireside Book of
Baseball *and other anthologies.*

*When his daughter flashes an aptitude for playing the point,
the writer begins to miss the point entirely.*

THE DAUGHTER YOU HAVE

~~~~~~

R. D. Rosen

I think of it as the Parents' Epiphany. It comes to all of
us parents sooner or later, but usually later. Almost
always a little too late, although we have only ourselves
to blame. After all, the Parents' Epiphany is usually pre-
ceded by countless Parents' Epiphany Opportunities,
any one of which could have become the Parents'
Epiphany if only we hadn't been so busy being Pre-
Epiphany Parents.

Take me and my younger daughter Isabel. She
showed unusual athletic promise, even as a toddler. She
walked confidently at nine months, had great hand–
eye coordination, and was fearless, occasionally to the

detriment of her physical well-being. As she grew older, and to my delight—since it was a trait that defined me— Isabel had a nose for the ball. She belonged to that minority of children who, in any game involving a ball, felt that they have a special claim on it. She ran after balls, dove for them, and occasionally wrestled them away from other children.

Let me just stop here for a moment to say that while an athletic son will almost surely rekindle a father's expired dreams, a man without a son will cling to a sporting daughter's potential for dear life precisely because he has no son. She is his last chance to shine vicariously before being dragged down by time's undertow. Being invested in a daughter's athletic ability comes easily to us, partly because we are free of sticky, competitive, father–son feelings. Our wishes for our daughters are uncorrupted by jealousy and ambivalence.

I wanted nothing more than for Isabel to use her gifts. The sport that caught her fancy turned out to be basketball. In her Saturday girls' basketball league, which she began at the age of eight, she glided up and down the court, dribbling with either hand, squinting at the tangle of players to find someone open for a pass. Her shots went in with what passes for regularity at that age. On defense, she fastened herself to her opponents, then picked their pockets as deftly as Walt Frazier. I remember her at ten being tailed closely on a breakaway following a steal. Without ever having practiced the move, she pulled up short near the basket and then calmly waited for her opponent to fly by before she swished a short jumper. The icing on the cake was that she never celebrated her little triumphs; she seemed above being surprised by her skills or needing to embarrass others. During the years I coached her basketball team, I frequently got frustrated with the team, the refs, the athletic limitations of a group of nine-year-old girls far more concerned with their ponytails than their passing lanes, but I was rarely upset with Isabel, who, as sweet-natured as she was, played with that quiet intensity you simply cannot teach.

It's essential to this story that you know that her interest in basketball coincided with my own basketball renaissance. I joined a long-standing basketball game of older men that convened once a week in Sandy Koufax's old high school in Bensonhurst, Brooklyn, an hour from my Manhattan home. Not only were most of the participants former players and coaches—the kind of men from whom I could learn skills that had eluded me growing up in a Midwestern town where there was no real basketball tradition—but our game was played according to a strict set of rules designed to prevent injuries and prolong everyone's playing career. Although I was the envy of all my friends with bad backs and knees, I knew I had long since reached the limits of my potential. Inside, I was busy converting my own limitations and feelings of mortality into more expectations for Isabel.

Expectations came easily. Isabel possessed three enviable intangibles. First, she had composure. Second, she could see the floor. Third, she was tough. After being knocked to the basketball court by some ten-year-old giantess, she'd pick herself up without complaint and proceed to steal the ball from her on the next play, then dribble the length of the court for a layup. Her vengeance had a cool, Clint Eastwood–like quality.

Actually, she had a fourth intangible, and it's interesting that I forgot it, since its absence in my own character cost me athletically. Isabel was eminently coachable—even by her flawed father. While I pontificated about the usefulness of bounce passes or playing defense by adopting the novel approach of placing oneself *between* the opposing player and the basket, most of her teammates looked blankly at me, endlessly resecuring their ponytails with scrunchies. Isabel, bless her heart, not only listened, she did her best to implement my instructions.

Naturally, it wasn't enough to enjoy these moments for what they were. Although it was a psychological disservice to all concerned as well as a cliché, I entertained images of watching Isabel, at some point down the road, play point guard for a small college. But to hide these crimes of parental hubris, around others I affected a pleasant indifference to my daughter's early success on the basketball court. I imagined that I had fooled her too.

It's ridiculous, when you think about it, that we expect our own offspring to be untouched by any of the struggles and anxieties that plagued our own childhoods—and that, in many instances, continue to define our adulthoods. Our children are the *last* people we should expect to escape the enviro-genetic web we've spun for them. Yet, at the first sign that children might surpass us in some even tiny aspect of athleticism, we can't wait to project onto the kid every stupid, vainglo-rious, and long-ago-discarded sports fantasy we ever in-dulged in for ourselves.

As an eighth grader, she started at guard on the junior-varsity squad of a small private school, and as a fresh-man she started in the varsity backcourt. As quick and aggressive as ever, she added a sweet one-handed set shot. My fantasies proliferated. The ball had beautiful rotation, but the arc was a little flat, hurting her field-goal percentage. I asked her to come to the playground so I could reengineer her release point and follow-through.

When she declined, I felt personally insulted, as though my interest in her basketball playing had been a down payment on some happiness she now refused to deliver.

Just for half an hour, I said.

No, thanks, she said matter-of-factly, as if I had of-fered her more zucchini instead of a chance to elevate her game. Why in the world wouldn't she want to work on her release and follow-through? Her teammates needed her outside scoring. I said, *But don't you have a responsibility to your teammates?*

That's okay, Dad. I just want to hang out with my friends.

I was like a wounded animal. *Half an hour—c'mon.*

I'll work on it in practice.

Undaunted, I mimed a release, making sure to leave my hand in the gooseneck position for her to appreciate. *If you groove a better release, you'll see—your shot will really start to fall.*

She smelled blood and went in for the kill.

I don't care, Dad. Sorry.

Wait. Had I missed the official notification that Isabel didn't really care about her shot? I knew she wasn't a jock through and through. I had by now seen other girls with "small-college guard" written all over them—a little quicker and a little tougher and a lot hungrier than Isabel. I understood my daughter had a lively social life, a new interest in photography, a passion for rock music, a genius for vintage-clothes shopping. But surely that left time to work on her arc, didn't it?

I felt like that defender four years before, chasing her down the court on a breakaway, only to have her stop on a dime while I sailed past, looking foolish.

It's okay, Dad. Some other time, okay?

C'mon, Isabel. We can work on your crossover dribble. Your reverse-spin move.

Dad!

It's hard for a father not to sound sexist here, but it is highly unlikely that any fourteen-year-old boy in her position would not want to work on his shot on his own. For boys, athletic success is one of the chief currencies of self-esteem, mastery, and popularity. I had played baseball into college before I hit the fork in the road and took the path marked "Writing" instead of the one marked "Caution: Can't Hit the Curve." It was hard for me to accept the fact that she had unilaterally renegotiated the terms of our unspoken agreement.

Okay, sweetie. I said. *That's fine. Don't worry about it.*

I could hear the air hissing as it went out of my little dream for Isabel. Which is to say, my dream about me.

And that was my first real Parents' Epiphany Opportunity—one of those moments that are the precursors of all the even tougher moments when you will have to understand the difference between the two of you, leave her alone, look the other way, and otherwise watch as she stands on the other side of the heartbreaking abyss between parent and child that is there for a reason. I got it, but I didn't.

As I said earlier, it takes most of us a little while.

So that's me lounging in the bleachers at her high school games. I'm the one who seems to have Tourette's, suddenly erupting with excitement at a good defensive play, spouting praise, or unleashing an epithet at an errant pass or bad call. Then, as I become aware that other parents are looking my way, alarmed at the sound of my voice in the mostly empty gym, I sink low in the bleachers, trying to hide from my own passion.

Before I know it, I'm in the dream again. Sketching plays on restaurant napkins over dinner with her. Chatting about defenses with her coach before the game. Telling Isabel to keep it out of Mindy's rocklike hands.

But the competition has stiffened, and Isabel can no longer prey so easily on unsuspecting ball handlers or get off her shot uncontested. She, too, throws the ball away. Her intensity is not enough to carry the team. She needs more arc on her shot.

I'm only doing this for you, she says chillingly one day.

Doing what?

Playing basketball.

This can't be true. I've never demanded she play basketball. Never berated her, like some fathers. Okay, I've offered my constructive criticism on a few thousand occasions. But I had put her in a league and she had found some joy there. She couldn't be faking it. What am I not seeing?

Tell me you're kidding, Isabel.

Okay, I am. But stop annoying me, Dad. Okay? And taking it so seriously.

One night—she's a junior now—I finally convince her to go to the Y with me to work on her shot. I am at once delighted and cringing at my own persistence. She listens to my suggestions, then shoots without enthusiasm. I long for an experience she will not provide.

After another shot with not enough arc hits the front of the rim, Isabel looks at me with ennui. Like I've dragged her to the museum, not a basketball court.

But I keep dreaming. During a playoff game not long after, I see her do something that astounds me. Trapped on the sideline with the ball, she wisely calls time-out. The referee blows his whistle and, as Isabel starts for the huddle, she coolly bounce-passes the ball behind her, *without looking,* right into the ref's hands. It's the confident, almost too cocky gesture of an experienced player—like flipping the bellboy a silver dollar—and I smile at her mastery of the game's nuances. Also, she's now referring to herself as a "baller."

A *baller*! It's a sign! There's still hope!

Except that when I look up "baller" on urban dictionary.com, I find that, although it originally described a thug who made it out of the ghetto to make millions playing professional basketball, it now refers to "any thug who is living large."

I, however, am living the small life of a parent who, to quote one of my favorite Zen aphorisms, is not riding the horse in the direction that it's going. Around this time, I turn to one of those books I keep near the bed to console and enlighten me, *The Parent's Tao Te Ching: Ancient Advice for Modern Parents*. Nearly everything in it makes me weep with a mixture of regret and hope.

> A pot has beautiful sides.
> The emptiness
> makes it useful.
> Empty yourself of agenda
> and you will be available
> for your children.

I do my best to unload agenda during the summer before her senior year. I bend over backward to prove I'm not holding agenda.

Isabel, I tell her in September, when she seems ambivalent about playing another season, *it's fine with me if you don't play.* I wonder how convincing I am.

I like playing on the team, Dad. And I work really hard in practice. I just don't like working on my shot when I don't have to.

I'm now ready to let this sink in. Basketball is an important social experience for Isabel; it's being part of the group that has meaning. For boys, the camaraderie is also crucial but not entirely divorced from the team's success. In fact, they have a synergistic relationship. It wasn't true for Isabel anymore—and, in fact, I don't think it had ever been true. For her, it wasn't who won or lost, or whether she put any more arc on her shot, but *that* she played the game.

I stopped asking her to work on her shot, and a cer-

tain sadness settled in during her last season. I was ending a relationship, the one I'd had for ten years, not with
Isabel, but with her basketball playing.

Look at your children closely.
You will never know the mystery of their being.
Can you love them still?

I'm the son you never had, Isabel tells me one day
when, against my better judgment, and because it is a
long road to the Epiphany, I'm diagramming on a nap-
kin a move she might try making. I cannot let go, and I
know it.

Realizing that I've just diagrammed my last play for
her, I put the pen down and say, *No, you're the daughter I have.*

Live your own life. . . .
There is no need to live theirs.
They will do that wonderfully
by themselves.

These are beautiful words, but if you don't have a
child you love, you can't know how hard it is to live
your own life while letting your children live theirs. It's
harder than hitting two free throws with time running
out and the other team's fans waving those plastic noo-
dles to distract you. Someday, perhaps, Isabel will be a
parent herself and discover that one of the things parents of teenagers talk about all the time is how hard it is,
this insidious confusion about where your life ends and
theirs begins.

Isabel goes out the way she started. In her last game (she'll be going to a college that doesn't even *have* a basketball team), she slaps the ball out of an opponent's hands, grabs it, and starts downcourt for a layup. But she's older now, and the players are tougher, and the other girl's on her ass all the way down the floor. Under pressure, Isabel throws up an errant shot.

Isabel barely changes her expression, puts her head down, and runs back on defense.

Toward the end of the season, some New York Knicks tickets fall into my hands and I get to take Isabel to three games. We've seen the Knicks once or twice before, but now it feels different. Although I keep pretentiously pointing out some of the little things players are doing that she might have missed, I've pretty much emptied myself of agenda. I'm not trying to teach her things that I think she needs to know in order to be a better basketball player. I'm not secretly wondering how much she really cares about the game. I'm not even concerned that she's missed some life lesson that, in my view, basketball is particularly well equipped to provide. When she has romantic fantasies about two of the Knicks, I take them seriously.

It's a new experience.

For the first time we're on the same team.

R. D. ROSEN *has invented a word* (psychobabble), *won an Edgar Allan Poe Award* (Strike Three You're Dead), *coauthored three bestselling humor books* (Bad Cat, Bad Dog, Bad President), *and chronicled a true love story between a middle-aged man and a buffalo* (A Buffalo in the House). *He is a senior editor at ESPN Books.*

When BMX racing became part of the Olympic roster,
Jill Kintner's father had a vision of his daughter's future.
But it fell entirely on her shoulders—and a bum knee—to
make it come true.

LIFE CYCLE

Jill Kintner with Alyssa Roenigk

When I was a kid growing up outside Seattle with my dad, Peter, my mom, Janice, and my brother, Paul, I loved watching the Olympics. My favorite event was downhill ski racing. My dad had been a skier at the University of Washington and, just like him, I loved anything with high speed and a lot of action. Every two years, he would record the Summer and Winter Olympics on VCR tapes for me and I would watch them until the ribbon wore out. When I was twelve, I told my folks I wanted to go to the Olympics. I didn't think I could compete. I just wanted to go and watch in person. But even that seemed like an impossible dream.

Then, in 2003, the International Olympic Committee announced BMX was being added to the 2008 Summer Games. I'd raced BMX all my life and had accomplished most of my goals, so I was ready for a new challenge. I had parked my BMX bike a few months before that announcement and transitioned to gravity mountain bike racing. I put the Olympics out of my mind, and Pops and I focused our energy on learning and adapting to a new sport. By 2006, I'd won two world titles and two World Cup titles. So as the 2007 Olympic qualifying season approached, people started asking me if I was going to return to BMX to try and make the U.S. team.

I didn't have an answer. My dad thought it was the perfect opportunity, but I didn't know if I wanted to return to my roots. I didn't know if I could still hang with the best riders in the world after being gone for nearly five years. My dad knew I could. I had been racing a bike, just one with bigger wheels. Thinking about returning to BMX, I was reminded of the reasons I left. But he assured me that things would be better than I remembered. From the moment of that IOC announcement, he had a vision about watching me race in Beijing. He thought life would be amazing for me if I had a medal. He wanted me to be on the cover of magazines and in TV commercials, and he thought I could make a difference. I didn't believe yet, but he did.

By September of 2006, I still hadn't decided. I felt like I had left BMX in the rearview. But that month, Pops had a heart attack. It was his second, and this time he didn't make it. He was my support system and number-one fan, and now he was gone. Losing him broke my heart into a billion pieces.

It took me gallons of tears to figure out how I was going to move forward and put those pieces back together. The Olympics had meant so much to him, and it began to mean a whole lot more to me. That winter, I went to the garage and fished out the bike I won my last BMX championship on and flew with it to Australia to spend time with my boyfriend, Bryn. While I was down there, I signed up for a few races to see how I felt being back on the bike. I wasn't perfect, but I felt pretty good.

The next May, I showed up for a qualifying race in the States. I wasn't fully prepared going in, but I didn't have expectations either. Honestly, I didn't care if I finished last. But I didn't. I won. That was the turning point. It opened a lot of eyes, especially my own. Right then, I knew dear ol' Dad was with me in spirit, chuckling away like he always did when he knew he was right.

Usually, at moments like those, he was the first person I called. But that was the bitter to the sweet this time. I had a lot of conversations with him by myself to fill that void, because I still wanted him to know what was going on in my life. I could almost hear his responses in my head. When I would call him, he had this special way of answering the phone that was just for me.

"Oh . . . hi-ya, Beanie!" That was his nickname for me, short for Jillybean.

"Hey, Pops. What's happenin'?"

After he died, sometimes I called my uncles instead. They sounded like him. I'd go over to visit and listen to them for hours. They resembled him, and their same quirky tendencies made me smile. They still do. And they knew I needed their support to get through that year. They would tell me stories about my dad—things

I'd never known. About his childhood and how he had talent as a skier, but not the opportunity or support of his parents. That's one of the reasons why he wanted so badly to let Paul and me know how much he and my mom supported us.

I did want to make the Olympic team. Not just for him and not just for me—for both of us. This was *our* dream. So I got serious. In the past, I had raced without any sponsor support and for very little money. This time, I landed a few major sponsors and a new coach and moved into the USOC training facility in Chula Vista, California. I had a place to live and train, access to coaches and a psychologist, and people who believed in me. Pops was the only piece missing. After that first race, I wrote "For Dad" on my shin guards and gloves. It was a reminder of the lessons he'd taught me and a way to carry him with me on my journey.

That season wasn't easy. During a training session in December, I ruptured my ACL and tore the meniscus in my right knee. I went through serious rehab, which kept me riding. But toward the end of March, I crashed again, and this time I *severed* the meniscus in the same knee. I had surgery the next day. The timing couldn't have been worse. The Olympics were only five months away, and I missed several of the qualifying races because of those injuries. But I wasn't about to stop. I put off the ACL surgery until after the Olympics and raced the rest of the season in a brace and in pain.

Had I called my dad then, asking for his advice, I think we would have talked about the lifetime of hard work we put into BMX racing. I understood what it meant to grit my teeth and work hard. And I was so close to the finish line. I couldn't give up.

The next month, I flew to Taiyuan, China, for the World Championships. It was the final race to decide which woman would represent the United States in Beijing. I was three weeks out of surgery and needed to place sixth or better to overtake my teammate, Arielle Martin—who was riding strong and confident—in the point standings. In so many ways, it didn't seem possible. So much needed to go my way that day. I wished I could talk to my dad, hear him tell me, "Beanie, go big or go home," like he always did. Instead, I closed my eyes, took a deep breath, and dug deep.

That day was a miracle. I could barely walk, but somehow, someway, I made it to the final and finished sixth. I had earned my spot as the only American woman who would represent U.S. BMX in Beijing—by one point. After an entire season of qualifying races, and after missing five of them, I'd made the team by one point. The stars aligned that day and that season. I think Dad did his part.

Losing my dad made me realize that everything we'd been doing as a family since I was eight years old—all the time spent driving to the track, tinkering with my bike, crashing and getting back up—it was all building up to this moment. I didn't see it before. But it was so clear to me after the World Championships. Every choice, every decision, every sacrifice—it was all done with a purpose.

In Beijing, I dedicated my racing career to my dad. Standing on the podium after the finals with a bronze medal around my neck was unbelievable. I still don't know how it all happened. That moment would have meant the world to him, and I wish he could have been there to see it. That was *our* moment, and I will cherish it forever. For Dad.

JILL KINTNER *is a three-time mountain-biking world champion and the 2008 Olympic bronze medalist in BMX. Born in Burien, Washington, she now splits her time between Seattle and Blue Mountains, Australia.*

How does high school softball compare to getting up close and personal with the Splendid Splinter and the Larry Bird—era Celtics? For one Boston-area sportswriter and his two daughters, it isn't even close.

MUDSLIDE

~~~

Dan Shaughnessy

*T*he catcher was born first, a mere fourteen months ahead of the centerfielder.

Sarah and Kate. Softball Sisters 4 Ever.

They came to sports at an early age. Their dad was in Milwaukee, drinking beer with Kevin McHale on the eve of Game 4 of the 1984 NBA Eastern Conference finals, the night their mom went into labor for the first time.

Sarah made a road trip with the 1985–86 Celtics (50–1 at home, greatest team ever) when she was not yet two years old. The Celtics flew commercial in those days, and Sarah was passed around as Larry Bird, Bill

Walton, Dennis Johnson, and the rest of the team flew from Boston to Detroit. Walton's head was larger than the catcher's entire body.

Kate was first to play softball. While her older sister skated and dreamed of following Nancy Kerrigan to the Olympics, Kate learned to hit, catch, and throw.

Everything was put on hold when Kate was diagnosed with leukemia at the age of eight. This brought a lot of ballplayers into her life, including Ted Williams—who for more than a half century was New England's guardian angel of sick kids. A week into treatment at Children's Hospital in Boston, Kate picked up the phone and heard the booming voice of the Splendid Splinter.

"Daddy, there's a loud man on the phone telling me everything's going to be okay," she reported from her hospital bed.

A few months later, Kate sat in the first-base dugout at Fenway, learned the two-seamer grip from Roger Clemens, then threw out the first pitch before a Red Sox–White Sox game. Kate never let go of the baseball/softball. And until Ted Williams died in 2002, every time I talked with him he had one question he wanted to know about Kate: "Can she hit?"

Kate can hit. Ted would have liked her swing. It's got that slight uppercut he wanted to see. She played Wiffle ball at the beach. She went to the batting cages. Like Ted, she had no time for teammates who weren't serious about playing. Her idea of makeup is a little eye black for those sunny days in the outfield.

Kate's older sister gave up skates for cleats when she was ten, and her first baseball was with a team of ten-year-old boys. She wasn't a catcher then, but she was fearless. She was also hitless until the final game of the season, when she surprised a boy—and herself—by ripping a line drive back through the box for a single in her final game of hardball.

It was softball after that, and she liked the position behind the plate. It's a place for leadership, toughness, and nonstop action. Soon the catcher was going to clinics and playing winter softball indoors with her sister. She got her own set of shin guards, not a typical accessory for a teenage girl. She blocked the plate like Johnny Bench, and there seemed to be at least one home-plate crash in every game. She had a whopper bruise on her left arm for senior prom. What color corsage matches a hematoma?

Separated by a single grade, the girls were teammates for three years in high school. This made the games all the more enjoyable for Dad, in the last row in the back corner of the aluminum bleachers on the third-base side. A sportswriter father always knows exactly where things stand regarding the lineup. You know how many batters will hit before your kid comes up next. When you've got two daughters in the batting order, you're pretty sure one of them is coming up every inning.

My place of business, *The Boston Globe,* does a pretty good job covering scholastic sports and still runs a couple of pages of agate type listing "league leaders" on spring Tuesdays during high school baseball/softball season. There was a proud moment in the spring of 2002 when the list of batting leaders in the Bay State Carey Division featured "S. Shaughnessy . . . .441" a

few lines above "K. Shaughnessy . . . .333." Doubt anybody else noticed, but it reminded me of the Alou brothers when I was a kid, and I still have the yellowed clip
tucked into a file in my home office.

I go to games for a living but enjoyed my kids' games
the most. Nothing beats the exuberance, camaraderie,
and lessons learned in high school sports. The girls had
team dinners and sleepovers at one another's homes during the season. Some days they would all go to school
wearing pajamas. They made up T-shirts for themselves
and their coach. Parents brought food to the games.

On the catcher's eighteenth birthday, she took a perfect, game-saving throw from her centerfielder sister,
tagged out the runner, and sent the game into extra innings. They won it in eight against the crosstown rivals.
Beat that for an eighteenth birthday.

In their final high school game together, they played
in the state tournament at home against Cambridge.
They fell behind, 8–2, then slowly came back. It started
raining fairly hard for their final at-bats in the bottom of
the seventh, still trailing, 8–5.

The catcher led off with a single to left. It was raining
harder. She came around to score on a couple more hits,
and it was 8–6 with runners on first and third and one
out. The centerfielder was coming to the plate when the
car-wash rains came. The umpires took the teams off
the field and agreed to give it a half hour.

Thirty minutes later, the rain had subsided, but the
field was under several inches of water. There was no alternative. Act of God. Cambridge wins.

The girls, all soaking wet and muddy, some with

big-league eye black running down their faces, hugged and cried. Then they smiled.

Pause. Somebody looked out at the field of streams and said, "At a time like this, there's only one thing to do—mudslide!"

They gleefully circled the swampy base paths and slid on their bellies across home plate. Coaches too. There was a giggling pigpile of drenched, muddied teenage athletes, laughing till they cried. Many had just played the final organized game of their lives.

It was a picture of competition, sportsmanship, and the sheer joy of high school team sports. Right up there with Celtics–Lakers, Patriots over the Rams, and the biblical Red Sox run in 2004, it ranks with the greatest sports moments I've witnessed.

DAN SHAUGHNESSY *is a sports columnist at* The Boston Globe, *where he has worked since 1981. He is the author of eleven books, including* The Curse of the Bambino *and* Senior Year: A Father, A Son and High School Baseball.

*A slip of the hand, a tenth of a point—that's all it takes
for an Olympic dream to fail. And to get passed down
to the next generation.*

HER TURN

George Vecsey

She kept loose to her opponent's music. She took a peek at the tiny Chinese girl out on the mat. She shimmied to keep warm. She took another peek.

Nastia Liukin had so many pulls in so many directions—the rival on the mat; her roommate and her friend, Shawn Johnson, who would compete last; and her father, her coach, whose gold medals she admired in their home in Texas.

Her immediate job was to not lose her mind in the waiting. Her father has told her how an Olympic gold can be lost for the tiniest mistake. In 1988 Valeri Liukin moved his hand in the wrong direction for one split second and lost the all-around gold by one-tenth of a point—to a fellow Russian. This need to be perfect has been drilled into her, since birth, really.

So she shook herself on the sidelines, in her pink outfit, her favorite color, and she eyed Yang Yilin, the Chinese gymnast who seemed like a sprite as she twirled around the floor. Arms akimbo, Nastia Liukin awaited her turn.

"I was watching, but my father always told me I can't concentrate on anybody but me," she said later. "I knew I had to do my normal routine."

Liukin maintained the cool she had displayed on the edge of the mat, and on Friday she defeated Johnson by six-tenths of a point for the all-around gold medal that had eluded her father. She celebrated with the poise of a young woman who had been preparing for this for all of her eighteen years.

The gold medal goes back to 1988, to the Summer Games in Seoul, South Korea. Valeri Liukin was a loyal gymnast for the Soviet Union and Anna Kotchneva, now his wife, was a rhythmic gymnast who did not qualify for the Soviet Olympic team. Valeri won two golds and two silvers, but he would never forget how close he came to his teammate, Vladimir Artemov, in the all-around competition.

"Close," Valeri Liukin said Friday. "Nothing to be ashamed of." As it happens, Artemov's son, Sasha, is also an American, and competed in the men's all-around final on Thursday, finishing twelfth. Now the Liukins have an all-around gold medal.

The lost gold was part of the family legacy, even when the couple moved to Texas and Valeri began coaching youngsters, including their daughter. Yesterday, Anna Liukin stayed away because of her fabled nerves—"she's chicken," Valeri joked—and the daughter stayed calm. Then father and daughter celebrated.

"She's very sensitive," the father said of the daughter, in the scrum of a mixed zone, one of the designated interviewing areas. "That part comes from her mom. I try not to be father, but after practice I am father. It's not easy. I am not going to lie."

He said he was watching his daughter while Yang, who is said to be fifteen, was performing. "I can see the tiger," he said of his daughter. "Her job, she did it."

Soon the daughter made her way through the mixed zone, and the father deferred, moved on. She had a gold medal. She could speak for herself.

"I knew I would have to go for it," she said. "I wasn't thinking about whether I could make it, but how I could make it. This is what my father taught me."

There is evidence that gymnastics, and perhaps all youth sports, have their dark side, with domination by coaches, harsh training practices, perhaps dubious ages for some of the tiny Chinese athletes. But Liukin and Johnson showed more than normal maturity for their age, telling how they had willingly shared a room at the athletes' village this past week.

"It's never been awkward for us," Nastia Liukin said. She also praised Yang for performing well, with the entire nation rooting for her.

"I can't imagine the pressure," Liukin said.

A Russian reporter asked the father and daughter to speak about their double heritage. Nastia went first, speaking in English, saying she represented the United States and adding: "I feel a little more American than Russian, but I'm very proud of being Russian and every year I go back to visit my grandparents and I feel more Russian, until I speak Russian. Why do I speak so badly? I feel I represent both countries."

Valeri spoke in Russian, saying: "I love America. I don't think I could have achieved so much in the Russia of fifteen years ago. Impossible. But we love Russia very much." The journey took a husband and wife to a new land. Now their daughter has a gold medal.

"This is a dream come true for both of us," Nastia said, including her mother. "I couldn't be more thankful." Then she referred to the all-around gold medal her father had sought twenty years before.

"My dad was so close," she said. "I hope I made up for that."

Valeri Liukin, sitting alongside his daughter, perked up at the talk of his daughter's gold medal. He held two fingers in the air.

"I have two," he said. It was easy to see where the daughter's steel came from.

GEORGE VECSEY *has been a sports columnist with* The New York Times *since 1982 and has covered seven World Cups of soccer, six Summer Olympics, and four Winter Olympics. In 1986, he was privileged to cover the Goodwill Games in Moscow, where he gained a great appreciation for the Russian people and the importance of sports like gymnastics. A native of New York, he is married to Marianne Graham, an artist, and they have three children, all of whom have worked in the newspaper business.*

*There are times when pulling your aimless teenage
daughter out of the bright sunlight and into a darkened
bar is actually the right thing to do.*

OUR MADNESS

Jaime Lowe

Los Angeles is not a sports town—enthusiasm for
anything ball-related is usually inherited. Although
sometimes it takes a while for the gene to kick in. When
I started at University High, I wasn't really into sports. I
wasn't into showing up at school either. I wasn't really
into anything except for anxiety and insomnia and
being a social outcast. Maybe it wasn't quite so extreme;
I think I was just looking for something to do besides eat
Subway in my car at lunchtime. It sounds so sad to me
now—little shreds of lettuce falling into the cracked
vinyl of the emergency brake and resting there perma-
nently. Opting out just seemed easier than navigating

the cliques and drama of high school. Some days I'd watch movies at the mall, two in a row. When the weather was nice (most of the time), I'd go west on Santa Monica Boulevard in my rusted-out Honda, sucking in the sunshine and bopping (as dourly as possible) to a mix tape loaded with suicide songs (Nirvana had just released *Nevermind,* so flannel and tear-drenched eyeliner were fashion statements). One March morning I set out to kill time (only a year and a half till college!) and landed typically at the ocean's edge.

I sat next to the waves, breathing with the wind's current, each surge of salty water kissing my feet. It was at the beach that I collected calm, that I knew I was not really sad, not really popular, not really anything yet. I would walk toward the rocks, toward the pier, then to the promenade and, bored, I'd move on to my dad's law office to see if he wanted me to file something or had the urge to voice some concern over my ever-expanding free time. His reaction, which he continues to be blushfully proud of, was to scoop me out of my burgeoning madness and deliver me to an Irish bar that served a different kind of Madness, one of the March variety. There I was, staring at the ocean . . . and then a few minutes later I was sitting in a cavernous, dark, whiskey-drenched bar watching college ball on a beat-down Zenith at eleven in the morning when I should have been in pre-calc and running SAT drills. Sitting in a place that was still suffering from the night before somehow made me suffer less. And here was this oasis—a small flickering screen of bodies twisted in balletic grace, working so hard for the glorious possibility of being the one in sixty-four that's left standing. Here was a TV in a newly bleached bar showing me shining moments, one right after the other. It was a pixilated window into another world.

I will always love March Madness. I will always love college basketball. I will always like to observe moments of silence as March approaches in anticipation of a ritual that started with my dad at that bar. I believe in the holiday of the first Thursday and Friday of the tournament—thirty-two games of basketball, pure competition, upsets, marching bands, cheerleaders, and the saddest faces drowning in tangible loss (those seniors' faces fallen when the buzzer strikes . . . heartbreaking). This is a religion I can believe in, and it's one that saved me during my junior year of high school and has continued to save me every year since. It's a reminder of impossible hope.

On that morning we were reveling in the presence of California greatness. My dad talked about Jason Kidd like he was the second coming of Bay Area basketball, and he was. There was so much expectation in this little-boy wonder in 1993, Kidd's freshman year at Cal. I just saw his busted face of determination. He could have been blind and still seen the court. He was a star in the mold of Magic, and that was the kind of basketball player I was taught to idolize—a passer, someone defined by making plays rather than finishing. And there was Kidd, storming past Bobby Hurley and two-time defending champion Duke. Duke! Cal was beating Duke! And here we were, sitting in the bar, my dad ditching his law practice in favor of a gin and tonic and giving his teenage daughter a chance to discover that there's virtue in talent and team and rooting for something outside yourself. There I was, actually *caring*.

College basketball didn't fix high school, and Jason Kidd didn't rescue me from myself. It didn't make my relationship with my dad better or different. It just was a gracious, howling moment that I could revel in. I could see the virtue in wanting something and in dribbling past whatever obstacles were in the way. I could see the virtue of a bucket and a net and a clean, easy goal. Pass, score, team. I could see how Kidd used his star skills to elevate everyone else. Sometimes, you have to choose sides, go with a team, and let them take you away. Sometimes you have to take a month (the worst-because-it's-last month of winter, say) and live by your bracket and be excited by something completely beyond your control. Sometimes a distraction, an appreciation of someone else's beautiful skill, is all you need to return to life—not quite as sad as you were before, not quite as buried in flannel and black lipstick.

I go to college basketball games now and look at these young pimpled faces and think about what a huge burden they carry for me. They have to inspire me every year. They have to do something that my dad and I can talk about. They have to win, lose, foul, shoot, and live on the court in front of a million TVs. They have to create conversation for a country, and they have to be a parenting tool for a dad who doesn't know how to say, "It's okay that you don't like school. It's okay that you don't have friends. It's okay that you sit for hours in front of the waves just waiting for something to happen. You will always have *this*."

JAIME LOWE *is the author of* Digging for Dirt: The Life and Death of ODB (*Faber & Faber, 2008*). *She has traveled cross-country in an RV covering March Madness for* Sports Illustrated; *she's also written for* The Village Voice, Blender, Radar, Penthouse, *The Daily Beast,* Interview, *the* LA Weekly, *and* The Infrastructurist.

A sports reporter looks back over his career in order to figure out how best to turn his toddler into an athlete.

LESSONS LEARNED

—⁓⌇⁓—

Eric Adelson

I have skinny legs. So skinny, in fact, that the very first thing my college roommate said to me—even before "Nice to meet you"—was "You need to do some squats." I didn't argue. I've been doing squats for years now, and I'm proud to say I can push out three plates on the leg-extension machine. Sadly, another patron of the gym where I train can do five plates. Her name is Amy.

So I have no illusions of raising a sports prodigy. I just don't want my daughter to inherit my legs. I want her to get her mom's legs, because her mom comes from an Argentinian soccer-nuts family. Her mom is athletic. Steve Spurrier even gave her punting lessons at Florida and suggested she might be better than the kickers he had. So I rejoiced when my daughter, Hope, happened to be born on the day Hope Solo & Co. won an Olympic gold medal for the United States in August 2008. I celebrated because *my* Hope's legs were chunky—chunky enough to trap puffs in her fat rolls. And when it was time early in 2009 for me to take her to play soccer at Mommy and Me class, I dreamed big.

Playing soccer with infants is a little odd. Parents swing their baby into the ball, which seems somewhere between amusing and abusive. The babies appear like props for moms to get their frustrations out. One baby shut his eyes. Another giggled. My baby . . . cried hysterically.

After the next week's class—when we played again and Hope bawled again—I met privately with the Mommy and Me teacher to discuss my daughter's "problem." It felt like a parent–teacher conference. She suggested we sit out and *watch* soccer. Great. My six-month-old was already retired. There wasn't even a JV team of two-month-olds.

I decided we would show them. Everyone loves a comeback story. I got a ball, placed it in the middle of the apartment, and swung her into it. Hope cried.

It had to be me. I was the stay-at-home parent. I was the one with no athletic skill.

But I did have one advantage: the knowledge of what makes great sports parents. After a decade covering athletes and making sure to talk to as many of their parents as I could, I had found something surprising: The more a parent showed off knowledge about a sport, the less it actually helped the child.

The best example of this came at Michigan, which had two great quarterbacks a decade ago: Tom Brady and Drew Henson. Brady's father didn't seem to get heavily involved. He didn't seem like a quarterback guru or even an athlete. He was an insurance consultant who had studied to be a priest. He basically seemed like a normal dad. Henson's father, on the other hand, was a coach. He knew everything about sports. He was one of those dads who, when they started talking, gave the impression that they were miles ahead of you. And he probably was.

So when Brady struggled—to the point that he told his dad he was giving up on playing football at Michigan—he was left to figure it out on his own. When Henson struggled, and even when Henson did well, his father came to Ann Arbor and watched practice. A team manager had to be dispatched to shoo him away.

One guess what happened to Henson (washed out of the Yankees' minor league system, went back to football, and then washed out of the NFL, having thrown twenty career passes) and what happened to Brady (a Hall of Fame–caliber career with more than 2,500 NFL completions over ten seasons and three Super Bowl rings).

But the best example of what works and what doesn't came to me as I reported my book about Michelle Wie.

Both Wie's parents, B.J. and Bo, loved Michelle deeply. They were there for her at every turn—literally, as Michelle was sixteen years old before she played a round without them watching. And their support (and their incredible genes) helped bring her to the brink of greatness. But when it came time to delegate to experts in the golf field, they couldn't bring themselves to do it.

Caddies came and went, each feeling disenfranchised. One got so exasperated that he handed the bag to B.J. and told him to do the job himself. Another wound up doing nothing on the greens except tending the pin. Coaches had to teach Michelle aspects of the game and then unteach what her parents did to her after the lesson was over. Even William Morris, Wie's PR agency, ended up unable to make a single decision on her behalf. The website created for Wie by William Morris was never launched, because B.J. didn't allow it.

Michelle's mom was a phenomenal athlete herself. She shot in the sixties as a young golfer in South Korea. Bo's brother was a champion bowler. And B.J. was no slouch—tall and strong and able to pick up sports like basketball quickly. But Michelle was beyond her parents. And when she turned pro, she should have been turned over to pros. Her parents were experts at parenting, but not at teaching sports. The best athletes rarely are.

Of course, there are exceptions. The Manning brothers come to mind. So does Barry Bonds. But girls often feel pressure more keenly than boys do. They want to please others more than boys do. And they listen to their parents far more than boys. I saw this time and again with Michelle, who wasn't afraid to mouth off to her dad but showed less and less willingness to go against him as the stakes got higher. B.J. would go out to the greens before every tournament to chart the slopes and hand a scribble-filled book to Michelle to consult before putting. That couldn't have given her the confidence to make the right decision. How could she believe she knew better when her father always did?

Connecticut women's basketball coach Geno Auriemma, who knows a little about what motivates female athletes, always says that an athlete's greatest strength is her greatest weakness. For Michelle Wie, it was her parents. And their greatest strength as parents and their greatest weakness was their absolute certainty. They had no doubt, and they still don't. And for a long time that helped Michelle. Then it began to hurt her.

Some parents seem to get this. One of the first stories I wrote for *ESPN The Magazine* was about Chris Simms, Phil's son, who was then a top football recruit in New Jersey. I figured the biggest expert on Chris would be Phil, so I called him up. He said he would not comment on Chris, to me or anyone in the media. He was polite but firm. I was disappointed but impressed.

So maybe it's fine that I don't know anything about soccer. And maybe it's even better that I don't know anything about how to mentor an athlete. Maybe being weak in the knees will be my daughter's greatest strength. She can't possibly feel like her dad knows better—at least when it comes to sports.

Hope got over her "problem." She can swing with the other babies now. She even likes it . . . sometimes. She just needed to get used to being launched into an inanimate object. And when she comes to me to talk about her high school soccer team, and how she can get better, I'll resort to the time-tested response used by smart dads before me: "Go ask your mother."

ERIC ADELSON *is the author of* The Sure Thing: The Making and Unmaking of Golf Phenom Michelle Wie. *He wrote for* ESPN The Magazine *for ten years and is now a stay-at-home dad in Orlando.*

A controversial soccer goalie offers proof that any dad can be an inspiration.

FINDING HER WAY HOME

⌐⌐⌐⌐⌐

Kurt Streeter

*H*ope Solo seems invulnerable—tall, strong, good looking—until she speaks of her father. Then her voice shakes and her eyes glisten and you understand how she found herself in the middle of a storm late last year: the best female soccer goalie in America, kicked off the national team during the [2007] World Cup, scorned by her coach and teammates for speaking her mind.

On a recent morning in Hermosa Beach, Solo, twenty-six, still sweating after a tough practice, sits at a café. She speaks of reclaiming her career and of the coming Olympics. She speaks of last year's painful troubles. Weaving through all of this is her dad.

"He always said what he believed, no matter who he was talking to," she says.

This is a way of explaining what happened in Beijing last September, at the World Cup. She says her father would have understood why she spoke out about being suddenly benched before the biggest game she would have ever played. She's certain of this. Even if, while remembering her father, a mysterious man, she is uncertain of much else.

She's unsure, for instance, of the horrors he saw in Vietnam, or if what he saw in those jungles made him what he would become. He refused to talk about it. She doesn't really know why, when she was in grade school and living in eastern Washington, he walked away from his family. Johnny Solo didn't just leave; he left and decided to become homeless.

They'd always been close. Before he left home, he gave her a nickname, "Baby Hope," the sweetest part of his life. He had been her first soccer coach, and she'd grown up hanging on his every word. So it was that in those first few years, as he lived on the streets of Seattle, he kept in touch through weekly letters and she never lost her love for him.

"People said terrible things about my dad," she says, somber now. "I never lost faith."

In time, she would become a formidable athlete, one of the best high school soccer players in the nation, by 2001 an All-American at the University of Washington.

She was rangy and skilled. Just like her father, she was also aggressive.

She smiles, thinking of the knife he carried and how

he said he would be unafraid to use it if attacked. She chuckles, remembering how, when businessmen approached and offered money that he had not asked for, he'd puff out his thick chest and snarl expletives. He was too proud for handouts.

Their bond had a chance to grow while she was in college, both of them living in Seattle.

Refusing shelter, he lived just a few miles from her, sleeping in a green tent in an outcropping of woods a few miles from campus.

He made it to every home game, trudging toward her with a limp, wearing a thick, foul-smelling coat. She says she learned to get over the embarrassment. And she also found herself trudging toward him, in the woods where he lived, walking through the mud to his tent. They'd sit there for hours, eating macaroni and cheese she had made.

He told her to learn from his life, the good and the bad. Baby Hope, don't ever let go of your family. Baby Hope, believe in yourself . . . don't be afraid of anyone.

By 2005, she'd graduated, played in Europe, and had become the top goalie on the U.S. women's soccer team.

Her father's great wish was to watch just once from the stands as she played for her country. In 2007, with a game scheduled near New York, she arranged for him to come. He'd grown up in the Bronx. She didn't know much more. Finally, he was going to walk her through the streets he'd played in as a boy, sharing parts of his life he'd always held tight.

"Everything was set," she says.

It was June. She was in Cleveland. They spoke on the

phone. Goodbye, Baby Hope, he said, hanging up. Good-bye.

A few hours later, another phone call came. Solo listened as a voice on the other end said that Johnny Solo's heart had given out. He was dead.

She wasn't sure if she could play again. Then she stiffened her spine the way her father would have and went to the World Cup.

With the first game about to begin, between the goalposts, she sprinkled a portion of his ashes around her. She could feel him pushing her, and she played like it, bouncing back from an early rough patch, not giving up a goal in two straight games.

But before the semifinals against powerful Brazil, Solo's coach, Greg Ryan, pulled her aside and delivered a surprise: She was being benched. Ryan simply had a hunch about Briana Scurry, a hero of the seminal moment in U.S. women's soccer, the 1999 World Cup.

Sure enough, Scurry played against Brazil—and gave up four goals.

Maybe it was the emotional toll from her father's sudden death, laid bare by the benching. Maybe she just did what he would have done. For whatever reason, when reporters asked about watching the game from the sidelines, Hope Solo looked them in the eye and let loose: It was "the wrong decision, and I think anybody that knows anything about the game knows that.

"There's no doubt in my mind," she continued, "I would have made those saves. . . . You have to live in the present. You can't live by big names. You can't live in the past."

Watching from afar, I thought that this was refreshing candor from an athlete, that it was particularly good to see a female athlete speak with such force, and that a real team should be able to weather this kind of dissent.

But her coach and teammates thought Solo was being selfish. Despite her apologies and with the consolation game remaining, she was kicked off the team and sent home. Alone. It wasn't clear whether she would ever return to the national squad.

In fact, she has returned, welcomed by a new coach. Solo admits that there are still frayed nerves, doubts from teammates, and her own worries, but she's intent on regaining trust.

In October, she joined the team for a series of exhibition games against Mexico. She didn't play, but it was a start.

She kept pushing, keeping her mouth shut, playing well in a series of practices held recently in Carson. In March, at the Algarve Cup in Portugal, she started in goal again, helping lead the U.S. to a championship. Last week, in Mexico, she helped her team qualify for Beijing, not giving up a goal in a hard-fought victory over Costa Rica. The Olympics approach. China, this summer. She has dreamed of this for nearly as far back as her memory goes. She thinks of returning there and tears flow. It's her father, how she has missed him, how she wishes he were here to encourage her.

"All of this made me realize that I'm like him in so many ways," she says. "I'll always be proud of that. . . . Every game I play from now on, I'll feel him with me."

KURT STREETER *is a narrative writer and occasional sports columnist for the* Los Angeles Times *who focuses on everyday people living uncommon lives. He has also covered transportation and the LAPD for the* Times *and the inner city for* The Baltimore Sun. *He lives in Los Angeles with his wife.*

He's a charming, frequently absent, larger-than-life dad.
She chose to follow in his slipstream. Now, if they can just
avoid having to pick up the pieces.

FULL THROTTLE

⌁⌁⌁

Ashley Force Hood

My father, John Force, has been a race-car driver for my entire life. Though he was on the road for most of the year when my sisters and I were growing up, he certainly made up for being gone when he was with us. I have wonderful memories of our time with Dad at the racetrack and also away from it. Now as an adult competing against my father in the NHRA Full Throttle Drag Racing Series, the stories just keep getting better.

I always joke that I was literally at the races before I was even born, but it's true! There are pictures of my mom, Laurie, pregnant with me and mixing fuel or backing up the funny car at the track. This may be how my love of racing began. As a baby, I got to travel on the road with Dad, and his team became my family.

He would let me try on his race gear, like his helmet and gloves, and I would peek over the seats in the tow van with huge earphones on my head and cross my fingers that Dad would win. As my sisters and I got older, we began to realize how cool our dad really was. Our friends would come over on Sundays after church, and we'd swim all day and then, when the races came on TV, we'd run down in our bathing suits and towels and pile into the living room to cheer Dad on. Mom always joked that whenever she said Dad was home, we'd run to the TV.

I lived in my dad's race T-shirts and loved anything to do with racing. On Mondays we'd ride with Mom to the airport to pick Dad up, and the next couple of days would be a blast. He'd let us stay up late, eat ice cream for dinner, and sometimes even skip school because he wanted to spend time with us. Our friends would all want to come over when Dad was there, because we'd either dress him up, do his hair or makeup, or we'd play games where Dad was the wild man-eating lion and he'd chase us all over the house.

I have one particular memory of him throwing his back out while charging under a table after us. He was in a lot of pain, but we thought it was hilarious that the lion had gone down. My mom always let us have our fun, and then, when Dad would head off to the next race, she'd reel us in and get us back on schedule with school, homework, and normal activities. This was our life—it was a little crazy, but it was fun.

I remember one situation that could have turned out to be a really sad story, but my dad came through and completely made up for it. In the third grade, we had a Bring Your Father to School Day in honor of Father's Day. We were supposed to share what our dads did for a living and also show them what we'd been doing in school. My dad was out of town, of course, so while all my classmates brought their dads, my close friend let me share *his* dad for the day. My dad felt horrible about it, however, so when he got back home, he brought his entire racing trailer, race car, and crew down to Travis Ranch Elementary School.

His team unloaded the car, and Dad explained what he did for a living and let the kids who answered questions climb right into the car. Once other classes found out, everyone wanted to come see the race car. Dad and his team spent an entire day at my school so all the different grades could come out and see. It was basically a publicity appearance, but only for seven-year-olds. He absolutely made up for missing out on Bring Your Father to School Day!

Not all of my memories are so wonderful. I have a crystal-clear memory of being at the Pomona race when I was about six and watching my father get into a horrible crash. His car flipped end over end in the sand trap at the end of the racetrack. We rushed down to him, and when we got to the car, it was upside down and still on fire. No one was rushing to put it out and I became hysterical, crying and panicking that Dad was trapped in the car. What I didn't know was that he was already out and on the other side of the NHRA Safety Safari truck, doing an interview. My mom tried to calm me down, but I was too upset, so she finally had to pick me up and carry me over to him so that I could see that he was all right. After that, I really didn't believe that my dad could get hurt in a race car. There were fires and crashes all the time and he always walked away, so we never worried about him. We thought it was cool. It would be almost another twenty years before this would change.

In September 2007, my father had a horrific accident in Dallas, Texas, when his race car came apart at more than 300 miles per hour, collided with another car, and tumbled over a guardrail. I was at the end of the racetrack, waiting to do an interview since I had just won right ahead of him. There were TV screens that we were watching, and when I saw the accident I looked up and saw his car come sliding past us into the sand trap. I ran to the car and was shocked to see that he wasn't in it. It was only the front half of the car and the motor. That was one of the worst moments of my life, because as I looked up the track and saw debris everywhere, I didn't know where to go to find him. Someone picked me up in a golf cart to take me to where he was, and my heart sank as my mind raced. It was probably less than a minute, but it's amazing how your mind can fill with a million images when you know your whole life may be about to change.

I remember thinking that he would never walk me down the aisle, meet my future children, or irritate or yell at me again, and it was a horrible thought. All of these images of him from when I was growing up— when he got pulled over for trying to make us laugh by driving in circles, when he accidentally washed my pet fish down the sink and took apart the whole plumbing system to save it—flashed through my mind, and I wondered if I'd ever have a chance to thank him for all the good, bad, and funny times. Thank goodness, when we got to him he was already yelling at all the medics—it was the best sound in the world, because I knew it meant he was alive.

Dad went through many months of rehabilitation, but I'm proud to say that he's racing again, driving us crazy again, and, yes, even with two mangled legs and feet, he managed to walk me down the aisle for my wedding in December 2008.

I work for my father, I compete against my father, and, although we are very different personality types (he loves attention and I shy away from it), we are very much alike, because we love drag racing funny cars at more than 300 miles per hour. I may not have had the most normal childhood, but I had a great one: Although I didn't get to see my dad as much as my friends saw theirs, when Dad was around he left no question in our minds about how much he loved us. And that's what really matters. For all of the times that he put me into a panic with his race accidents, I made up for it when I got into a crash in Seattle and Dad ended up in the ambulance instead. I was absolutely fine, but Dad had to be taken away because he had a panic attack and couldn't breathe. He's always been a little overprotective. It's no different now than it was fifteen years ago, when Dad saw an ambulance in our hometown and followed it all the way to the hospital to make sure none of us was in it.

He's a crazy dad, but he's definitely a fun dad who

loves his family and racing more than anything else in the world—and that shows in everything he does. I hope for many more years of wonderful memories, both at the track and also away from it. And, come to think of it, we haven't put Dad in makeup in a while. That might be a fun project the next time my sisters and I have a weekend off. Knowing Dad, he'll do anything to make his girls smile. Even if it means wearing pink lipstick and curlers.

In only three seasons as a professional funny-car driver, ASHLEY FORCE HOOD has distinguished herself as one of the top drivers in the NHRA. The 2007 Auto Club Rookie of the Year and 2008 Jim Murray Female Athlete of the Year, she led the funny-car point standings in both 2008 and 2009. In April 2009, she reached 312.13 mph, setting the national speed record. That September, she became the first woman to win a funny-car title at the Mac Tools U.S. Nationals, the richest and most prestigious NHRA event. She lives in Yorba Linda, California, with her husband, Dan, and their cat, Simba.

*Once upon a miracle, goalie Jim Craig looked up into
the seats at Lake Placid to locate his father. Nowadays,
he looks down from the stands to watch his daughter
play hockey.*

THE OTHER SIDE OF
THE GLASS

Jim Craig

Kids face enough challenges when they participate in sports. It gets even more burdensome when they have a parent who achieved distinction in athletics.

My daughter, Taylor, felt the added pressure of competing in a sport in which her father won an Olympic gold medal.

Taylor was five when she first got on skates. It was play—kind of like kicking a soccer ball to nowhere in particular or running without a start or finish line. It was just for fun. It wasn't long, though, before she wanted to skate in a hockey game. Taylor wanted to compete.

My wife, Sharlene ("Charlie"), and I weren't in uncharted territory. Our son, J.D., who is three years older than Taylor, had taken up hockey when he was seven. We fully supported him, but we also wanted to make sure that the sport was something he wanted to do—not because his dad played hockey, but because *he* wanted to play hockey.

We taught J.D. that the game had to be fun and that the game was not about him, not about being Jim Craig's son playing hockey. It was about his team, his teammates, and teamwork. We taught and impressed upon Taylor the same lessons and outlook.

I encourage my children to play sports, any sport. It didn't make much difference what sport they played. All sports enrich the lives of kids and teach them life lessons. I feel the same about the value kids receive from painting, playing an instrument, acting, and running for and serving on the student council.

Taylor and J.D. acquired their own passion for hockey. Neither chose to play goal; both became forwards.

I thought early on—more with Taylor than with J.D.—that I had to be aware of and sensitive to my competitive nature and the intense focus with which I played. I remembered that I'd had mentors who inspired and pointed me in the right direction, but ultimately I was the one who arrived at and adopted my competitiveness and focus. Taylor had to find her own way as well.

I want sports to be an activity in which my children compete, understand teamwork and the value of being a teammate, appreciate and honor commitment and accountability, and make personal sacrifices. I want them to gain confidence through sports.

And I am always aware that there is a line that separates the pursuit of virtue in athletics and what can amount to undue and unhealthy pressure.

I wondered and treaded carefully in being a "hockey dad" to a girl. Would I be as in synch and sensitive to the needs of a daughter as I was to those of a son? Would I be too tough on Taylor? Not tough enough? Ask too little of her? Ask too much?

My relationship with my daughter, the hockey player, had added complexity in that I coached the youth teams she played on. How would I balance coaching my "little girl"? I was Taylor's biggest fan, but I also had to make the decisions that were ultimately best for the team and for Taylor.

Growing up in a tight-knit family of eight kids—which included three brothers and four sisters—had provided me with a valuable if incomplete education in understanding girls.

Once Taylor decided that she wanted to play hockey, Charlie enthusiastically supported her. Having Mom on board was especially helpful and important, since there was no local league for girls and Taylor would have to play in the boys' league. Girls' hockey leagues prohibit checking; the boys' leagues, starting at about the eight-year-old level, allow it.

In grade school, there isn't a big difference in physical strength between boys and girls. But starting in fifth and sixth grades, and definitely in junior high, guys begin to get stronger. Not tougher, just stronger. It is challenging

enough for boys as they get older to adapt to more physical and faster play; it would be even more difficult for
Taylor.

My daughter, the hockey player. When I was in high
school, girls playing organized ice hockey were almost
nonexistent. Parents worry about the well-being of all
their children. I got particularly anxious when Taylor
started to get hit on the ice. She didn't seem to mind the
collisions; it was her father who needed to toughen up.

⁓⁂⁓

Young women are just as emotional and fierce competitors as boys. And there is no "fairer sex" in hockey.
Girls play as hard and with as much determination as
guys do.

There are, however, differences.

A key difference is that girls' and women's hockey
doesn't command the media attention or the money
of the boys' and men's game. There's no professional
women's hockey league. Boys in youth hockey all have
fantasies of bright lights and big crowds and TV broadcasts and their faces on trading cards.

Right from the get-go, the cultures of boys' and girls'
hockey are different; the dreams and hopes and inspiration for girls playing hockey are more fundamental and
purer. They are more about the essence of skating and
passing, moving without the puck, camaraderie, making
friends, and playing for the love of the game.

As well, even though girls compete with the same
level of emotion and fierceness of intensity, I found in
parenting and coaching Taylor and her hockey sister-
hood that girl athletes have more delicate and subtle

psychologies. They are more open and less guarded than boys. Charlie was a necessary and indispensable tutor and partner in understanding these emotions and assisting me to be the best—there's that term again—"hockey dad" for Taylor.

She took to the game, and I learned as much from her as she did from me. Hockey brought us closer.

Taylor inherited the determination, fiery spirit, and competitiveness that underpinned my success in athletics and business. She was eager to get onto the ice and reluctant to leave it. She spent hour after hour on the ice and also out in the driveway, taking shots at a net she'd placed out there.

What also became apparent, fast, was that not only did Taylor enjoy hockey and work hard at improving, she also had ability to excel at the sport. As she started to earn her own reputation, I made sure to remind her that the game was not about her, not about whose daughter she is, but about being the best player she could be to help her team become the best it could be.

I wanted my successes in hockey to be a non-factor and did not want to revisit my own glories through Taylor. Indeed, one of my favorite quotes is "Never let your memories be larger than your dreams."

As a parent, you need to be aware that if you did big things in the arena, your kids aren't about providing a shout-out for the goals you scored or prevented, the passes you caught, or the races you ran all those years ago. Just as important, if Mom or Dad didn't win or make a name in sports, it isn't their son's or daughter's job to do it for them.

When Taylor was a freshman in high school, she chose to try out for varsity hockey: not the girls' team—the school didn't have girls' hockey—but the boys' team. J.D., a senior, was the co-captain of the team and played on the first line.

The decision was Taylor's, even if Mom and Dad may have had concerns about the ramped-up speed and increased size and strength of the competition, which translated to more-forceful checking and harder hits.

J.D., a protector of his younger sister, was less than thrilled about having to focus on the dual roles of being team leader and watching out for Taylor. Charlie and I could preach over and over to J.D. and Taylor that she was one of the guys if she chose to play with them, but in reality neither of her parents nor J.D. totally bought into this. Taylor was going to be something of a pioneer—never an easy task.

As in the past, things weren't made any easier by my being a coach of the team, this time in an assistant capacity.

Taylor made the team and soon found herself on the second line. Sometimes, when on the power play, for example, she would be on the ice with her brother. There were some accommodations that were made for Taylor, but not many. She got dressed in her own locker room, and once all her teammates were dressed and ready, she joined them in the boys' locker room for pregame instruction—as she did for instruction and coaching between periods and for the postgame talk.

Only a few games into the season, protecting Taylor was no longer front and center on J.D.'s radar screen. He now saw her primarily as a teammate, not his sister. She had earned J.D.'s respect for her play and what she gave to the team.

It was a fun season. J.D. and Taylor both played well. Taylor was a valuable contributor to the Tigers. As for the checking and hitting, yes, she took some lumps, but she dished them out too.

At the top of the list of Taylor's strengths and value to her team were her understanding, instincts, and feel for the game, her ability to "see" the action, her ability to move without the puck, and, when she had the puck, to be patient and make smart decisions. In my memory, I go back to a game in which she had the puck out near the point, and her sense of the play on the ice became apparent: She did not rush anything; she held on to the puck and studied the flow of players and allowed opportunity to develop.

Taylor and I began to have more in-depth and strategic discussions about hockey. What is particularly fun and productive about our talks is that Taylor seeks to learn about what's going on in the mind of the last defender she has to beat, the goalie, and what she needs to do to beat him or her. Having been that last line of defense, I try to provide my Taylor with as much information as possible to make the life of the goalie miserable.

―――――

Following that season, as the spring approached, J.D. got ready to graduate and do a year of postgrad at a prep school. Charlie and I decided that we wanted Taylor to attend Tabor Academy, an independent coeducational boarding school located on the south coast of Massachusetts.

Taylor had met big challenges. She needed to explore and take on still more.

We chose Tabor because of its excellence in academics and the overall community and extracurricular offerings, which include a strong girls' hockey program. Its girls' team plays one of the most competitive prep-school schedules in New England. Girls in this league go on to play college hockey at all levels. Many play on All-Star and regional teams; some play internationally.

Taylor applied to Tabor and was accepted. She's now a junior. What encourages me is that she works hard to optimize the value of the opportunities the school makes available to her. She works hard at academics, athletics, and being an involved and responsible citizen.

I see Taylor weekly, and I attend as many of her games as possible, but there's a separation that didn't exist when she lived at home and went to public school. It hasn't been easy—mostly for me. Taylor is growing up and establishing herself. Dads the world over can relate to my emotions.

She is becoming the beautiful, poised, and considerate person I hoped she would become—and hockey has played an important role in this growth.

I still coach an amateur team on which Taylor plays. Yet I have largely left that father/coach–daughter relationship. While the character of Taylor's relationship with hockey will always be affected and influenced by her dad having played for the 1980 U.S. "Miracle on Ice" team, her time on the ice is now far more independent of her dad the goalie.

Taylor is better able to concentrate on being one player on a team and doing her best to help that team win. This is just the way it should be.

She continues to improve as a hockey player. She's among the top players in her age group in the U.S. She played in her first international tournament, up in Canada, in the summer of 2009.

Of course, as Taylor faced tougher competition, it wasn't all winning and smiles and sunlit experience. It never is—not for anyone. Taylor had moments of doubt and anxiety, setbacks and defeats in hockey, just as she will in life. There will surely be more of this ahead. And it's here where I can be of specific help to her. Not much came easy to me, in hockey and in many other areas—I failed and was passed over and overlooked often—but I channeled that experience into positive energy. When Taylor confronts obstacles and approaches hurdles, this is the advice and example I recommend to her.

Helping Taylor in this way strengthens our bond.

It's a bond between father and daughter.

It's also a bond between hockey players.

During the 2008–09 season, J.D. and I were at the Westminster School in Connecticut, watching Tabor Academy play in the third sudden-death overtime of the semifinals of a prep school tournament. We took in the game from ice level, alongside the boards next to the glass on the Tabor offensive zone.

Taylor readied herself to take a face-off in the circle right on the other side of the glass from us. About three seconds prior to the referee dropping the puck, I saw that the player facing off against Taylor had no defender behind her. Taylor looked over to me at about the same time, and I signaled to her, a combination of a nod of my head and a hand gesture, which she understood—and an example of the bond we share.

The puck dropped, and Taylor allowed her opponent to win the draw and kick the puck back to the empty area where there should have been a defender. Taylor raced toward that spot, gathered the puck, and slipped it to a teammate, who put it past the goalie for the game winner that put Tabor in the tournament final.

Moments like that are about more than hockey X's and O's; they are also about love and dependability and sharing.

My daughter loves hockey much the way her father loves hockey. This makes me happy. I hope Taylor continues to play the sport and to enjoy it and to grow and become a better, more rounded person through it. I hope that hockey transmits to her lessons and values that she can apply to being a winner in life.

And when the day arrives that I am sitting in the stands at a rink, watching my daughter on the ice, and someone comes up to me and asks with earnest excitement, "Hey, aren't you Taylor Craig's father?" I will be proud, and not a bit surprised.

Olympic gold medalist JIM CRAIG *was the goalie for the 1980 U.S. "Miracle on Ice" hockey team. He is the founder and president of Gold Medal Strategies, a company that advises and inspires people and organizations to achieve their full potential.*

ACKNOWLEDGMENTS

This book actually owes a lot to the United States Congress. Without Title IX of the Education Amendments of 1972, which mandated equal opportunities for women, we would not have the richness of material contained in this anthology: stories about baseball, basketball, BMX, boxing, equestrian competition, funny cars, golf, gymnastics, running, soccer, softball, tennis, triathlon, etc. More significantly, the bonds between fathers and daughters might not be as strong without those and other sports.

There are people to thank besides politicians. Chris Raymond, formerly of ESPN Books, came up with the idea for the original *Fathers & Sons & Sports* book that led to this one. While not enlisting accomplished athletes and writers to tell their stories, Bill Vourvoulias and Steve Wulf found classic pieces worth reading again. Paul Taunton and Kelly Chian at Ballantine Books and Sandy DeShong and John Glenn at ESPN Books deftly navigated the book through the straits of editorial production. Karin Batten came up with a graceful interior design for the book, and Belina Huey is responsible for the handsome cover. Thanks also to Mickey Steiner, who helped track down dimly remembered articles based on only the sketchiest of information.

ABOUT THE TYPE

This book was set in Sabon, a typeface designed by the well-known German typographer Jan Tschichold (1902–74). Sabon's design is based upon the original letter forms of Claude Garamond and was created specifically to be used for three sources: foundry type for hand composition, Linotype, and Monotype. Tschichold named his typeface for the famous Frankfurt typefounder Jacques Sabon, who died in 1580.